Janez Juhant

From Ethical Person to Dialogical Society

Janez Juhant

From Ethical Person to Dialogical Society

Challenges of Global Society

LIT

Cover Picture: Anka Doblekar, Persons and Things
Copyright: Anka Doblekar

This book is printed on acid-free paper.

Bibliographic information published by the Deutsche Nationalbibliothek
The Deutsche Nationalbibliothek lists this publication in the Deutsche Nationalbibliografie; detailed bibliographic data are available in the Internet at http://dnb.d-nb.de.

ISBN 978-3-643-90415-7

A catalogue record for this book is available from the British Library

Zweigniederlassung Zürich 2013
Klosbachstr. 107
CH-8032 Zürich
Tel. +41 (0) 44-251 75 05
Fax +41 (0) 44-251 75 06
E-Mail: zuerich@lit-verlag.ch
http://www.lit-verlag.ch

LIT VERLAG Dr. W. Hopf
Berlin 2013
Fresnostr. 2
D-48159 Münster
Tel. +49 (0) 2 51-62 03 20
Fax +49 (0) 2 51-23 19 72
E-Mail: lit@lit-verlag.de
http://www.lit-verlag.de

Distribution:
In Germany: LIT Verlag Fresnostr. 2, D-48159 Münster
Tel. +49 (0) 2 51-620 32 22, Fax +49 (0) 2 51-922 60 99, E-mail: vertrieb@lit-verlag.de

In Austria: Medienlogistik Pichler-ÖBZ, e-mail: mlo@medien-logistik.at
In the UK: Global Book Marketing, e-mail: mo@centralbooks.com
In North America: International Specialized Book Services, e-mail: orders@isbs.com
e-books are available at www.litwebshop.de

Acknowledgements

I thank Vojko Strahovnik for his comments on my writings. I am also grateful to Erika Prijatelj for her precise and tiring proof-reading and copy-editing of this book. I owe my thanks as well to all others who support my life and my work. I appreciate my students and all those who test me, sometimes with their inconvenient comments/questions. This motivates and challenges me.

I thank the ARRS (Slovenian Research Agency) for the financial support required to produce this book. A part of this book was prepared within the research project Dialogue in the Global Multicultural Society (ARRS J6—4139).

It is difficult to find time to read a book, so authors try to invent the *nova*. This book brings out the *nova et vetera* (new and old treasures, Mt 13, 52)!

The author
Sora, December 2013

CONTENTS

INTRODUCTION

Life conditions for people are more challenging now than ever in the history of mankind.

The millennia old foundations of humanity are cracking. In the words of Jacques Monod (1990, 281) we are facing "a rejection of centuries old spiritual tradition where spirituality is a decisive source of knowledge". The development of modern society was stimulated by the downfall of the mediaeval order, which secured balance in an individual person and among all persons, in the societal order. The golden middle was the ideal for balance between body and soul (*ora et labora*), between the individual and society, between earth and heaven and between the outer and inner dimensions of life. The scientific and technical acquisitions of modernity stimulated human endeavour to perfect the outer conditions of life, which then resulted in the improvement of life's physical conditions. These occurrences emphasised that faith could be the solution to all human problems. The end result was that humans were strengthened in their faith and this provided security for life. Today this life approach has entered into a crisis, which in turn has become a touchstone regarding the capacity of human beings to manage his/her life issues.

Every human being is symbolic. To live he/she needs to enable his/herself to share his/her emotional life through experiences with others; initially these are the parents. Human language is the means. Language presupposes a dialogue among partners, which is not only a lingual but much more importantly an emotional exchange among them. The first years of life are particularly decisive. In these years a young person assimilates the codes necessary to perceive himself, others and through them the whole world. Dialogue is a person's basic task to organize their life and to act humanly. Children raised by animals have witnessed that children need personal relationships in order to develop the capabilities of a human person. The emotional dimension is more important than the grammatical-symbolic one. This basic human pattern will be repeated throughout a person's life cycle. The lack of this personal exchange among people is a decisive cause for aberrations within individuals and consequently within societal life.

Society grapples with variations of these problems in human life. Modernity primarily challenges individuals and society because both lack the conditions which allow opportunities for a personal exchange. An ethical praxis without a healthy emotional exchange is weak. It is difficult to become an ethically autonomous person, able to communicate ethically, able to enter into relationships and able to solve his/her own problems and those of others.

The fringes of modern society and the most recent crisis we are facing are consequences of the absence of dialogical conditions among people. Dialogue is a challenge for philosophy, religions and sciences. Philosophers estimate dialogical method to be the ground for solving the basic questions of life. Religions stressed and continue to stress dialogue with God to be a precondition of good dialogue among people. In modern times science is present more and more only in selected spheres of human life and the world. This became one of the central reasons for the modern crisis. Dialogue among philosophies, religions and sciences is a way toward a global empathic society. This is a path toward a good art of life – an improved quality of life - and also a willingness to give one's life for the sake of others. This can be accomplished only through the capacity of deeper insight into the mysteries of people. We face each other as competitors and struggling on behalf of our own interests we are often ready to exclude others. Scapegoating mechanisms prevail and others become victims of our desires. The corporeal desire is on the one hand a motivation for people to act and on the other it is a cause of rivalry and exclusion. The culmination of these victimisations is the crime of totalitarian systems. The enormous scope of human rights violations was the consequence of tensions in modern liberal societies. Are we able to overcome this simulated crisis and to end the manufacturing of more and more victims? Genocide and suicide are the consequences of a lack of dialogue in modern society as well as the loss of humanity's ancient values. Are we able to overcome this emptiness and to establish a virtuous society moving toward an empathic society?

The Appendix is an attempt to deal with the Slovenian Theologians.

1. POST-MODERN CONDITIONS OF PERSON AND CHRISTIANITY

Changes in the post-modern world

The aim of this discussion is to consider some dilemmas of the modern world, which result in attempts by the *currents of post-modernity* to solve these conflicts. In these efforts Christianity and Christian churches play a key role. With consideration of modernity's theoretical and social changes, we will try to identify the dilemmas of the Catholic Church. As the Church has noticeably participated in shaping the processes of modernity she remains dependent upon these processes.

The processes of modernity paved the path for the present globalisation. From the sociological perspective globalisation is synonymous with the interconnectedness of the modern world. Since globalisation is principally determined by financial-economic lobbies globalisation confronts person and society with a new challenge. Humanists from different roots and perspectives work to overcome it. Postmodernism is a new era of dialogue. It stems from heterogeneity of the global world and is likewise confirmed by the world's antagonisms. From a geographical perspective the Catholic Church is recognised as a remarkably globalised institution. Therefore it is capable of playing a major role in these processes.

However, the process of free governance can be viewed as the biggest challenge in the Church's history. If the Church wants to retain its active role in world development it will necessarily demand certain adjustments (Beck 2000, 243, 261). According to Beck, "the Catholic Church is a post-modern response to the second modernity. More carefully stated: It (the Church) could search its pre-modern memory for organisational forms, ideas and answers for the second modernity (post-modernity) and offer something which many find indispensable for thought and action under the conditions of globalisation." (Ibid. 275)

The Christian religion with its universal (Catholic) organisational foundation can be an important factor in solving the problems brought about by globalisation. Christianity provided grounds for the crucial demands of post-modernity: concern for the individual, solidarity, subsidiarity and dialogue. As a pre-modern institution, the Church will either manage to appropriately transform itself and actively participate in shaping these processes, or it will become trapped into isolation by the post-modern challenges and thus miss the opportunity to take part in shaping the post-modern world.

Building united Europe on the ideological ruins of modernity and its technical-rational mind, as well as the post-modern search for a new mode of communication between people, nations, races and various other groups signify both demanding and lengthy processes. The predominantly economic globalisation dictates the pace of development and not everyone can keep up pace on an equal basis. Many are left behind. This explains why the modern world abounds with tension. The events of September, 11th in the USA are just a singular expression of this tension. Its foundations can be traced through the sharp contrasts of our world. These contrasts were made even more obvious by economic globalisation – accompanied and dictated by media: “Medium is a message”. Through media, the whole world becomes “the global village” (Marshall McLuhan [1911-1980]), 1989). On one hand, global village creates the feeling of opportunities for all. On the other hand, it imposes the mentality of rivalry. The globalisation of media enables the world's reality to be even more available to people. It offers itself and at the same time it is intrusive. The differences, which deprive individuals and groups of equal opportunities to access the world’s goods, become increasingly obvious. J. Rawls (1999). This raises the question of an individual's starting point.

The problem of inequality and exclusion causes tension and terrorism. The conspirator Osama bin Laden justifies: "Terrifying an innocent person and terrorising him is objectionable and unjust; also unjustly terrorizing people is not right. Whereas terrorizing oppressors and criminals and thieves and robbers is necessary for the safety of people and for the protection of their property. The terrorism we practice is of the commendable kind for it is directed at the tyrants and the aggressors and the enemies of Allah, the tyrants, the traitors who commit acts of treason against their own countries and their own faith and their own prophet and their own nation … Tyrants and oppressors who subject the Arab nation to aggression ought to be punished … America heads the list of aggressors against Muslims … For over a century, Muslims in Palestine have been slaughtered and assaulted and *robbed of their honour and of their property*” (Bin Laden 1998).

Every human person as a symbolic being is constantly determined by the existing, settled cultural patterns, which is accepted as he/she matures. While antiquity and the Middle Ages maintained a certain cultural consistency, the subjectivity of modern times opens the doors wide for the subject's gaze and brings into the old monolithic unity the variety established by subjective starting-points. This is the beginning of the modern era, the era characterised by the end of metaphysics and by the affirmation of the subject as an entity who autonomously reconstructs the world (Descartes: *cogito ergo sum*) along with its antagonisms (Vattimo 1997, 40ff.). Pascal perceives this as the greatness and misery of mankind (Pascal 2012, Nr. 397-8), which according to P. Valery lead into "crisis of spirit" (Valery 1957, 989). While the world was originally (according to Plato) governed by the concept of the Good (Plato, *Politea*, VI/19), to which every soul must submit and which comes from heaven that dominated the ancient Greek and medieval world, modernity transposed conceptual (or ideological) management of the world to the Earth, thus bestowing divine dimensions on the earthly. That is why modern ideologies appropriate the seal of sacredness (Bürger 2000, 55).

According to Plato, man as a thinking being has the ability to perceive and comprehend (Gr. *theoreín*), consequently, the Greek and medieval cultural frame thoroughly follows the guidance of the concept of the Good or God, and dares to explain the world only under its umbrella. German idealists were perhaps the last who tried to preserve this unity and autonomy of the subject by including man into the absolute order of will or freedom that is secured by God as the fullness of freedom (Kant, Fichte), or the fullness of knowledge (Hegel), but they themselves as well as other currents of modernity, especially science and technology as the driving force of modernity, threw open the doors to the revolutionary arbitrariness of the omniscient subject: “Science represented power, human power, but science could not address the question of how this power ought to be used.” (McAllister 1997, 163)

The troubles of Catholic Church in the modern World

The Catholic Church was forced to accept the modern logic of self-regulation. Through Neo-scholasticism, it rendered the Catholic idea operational to be competitive with the modern trends. The social-political engagement of Catholics in relation to some papal social circular letters

Rerum novarum (Leo XIII 2013/1891); *Quadragesimo anno* (Pius XI 2013/1931); *Mit brenender Sorge* (Pius XI 2013/1937); *Divini Redmptoris* (Pius XI 2013/1937) and the implementation of the so-called Catholic policy (Christian-Social or Democratic Party) were not of so much social relevance.

Parallel to and in competition with the modern will to power and control of the society, the Catholic Church, too, develops the strategy to control social space and sets up mechanisms for this control, which raises the question regarding the openness of social and spiritual space (Hollis 1994, X/2). Similarly as in the case of the rational-technical control of systems, the aforementioned control by the Church brings forward the problem of freedom. Just like the philosophical criticism of the modern manageability is placed within the absolute obedience to the concept of the Good (Plato), the Christian tradition offers analogous obedience to God as the only Guide: "Neither be called masters, for you have one master, the Christ." (Mt 23, 8-12) Since the Church is concerned with proclaiming God's reality, not with control and reign, any technical-rational or merely sociological availability is alien to it. The Holy Spirit provides, according to the Holy Scripture, the necessary freedom for the Church, and enables it to overcome any entanglements and limitations, since Christ brought this genuine freedom to the whole of creation: "...because the creation itself will be set free from its bondage to decay and obtain the glorious liberty of the Children of God" (Rom 8, 21). For this reason, the Church is, in accordance with the Second Vatican Council, in a state of constant renovation ("*semper reformanda*", cf. GS Nr. 41/2, 62/6 and 91/2, 92/2).

Modernity and total science as self-production

Modernity threw open the doors of the subject's productivity, this resulted from its means and foundations: science and technology as well as ideologies. As put by Izaija Berlin: "One is the development of the natural sciences and technology, certainly the greatest attention has been paid from all quarters. The other, without doubt, consists in the ideological storms that have altered the lives of virtually all mankind: the Russian Revolution and its aftermath - totalitarian tyrannies of both right and left and the explosions of nationalism, racism and, in places, religious bigotry, which, interestingly enough, not one among the most perceptive social thinkers of the nineteenth century had ever predicted." (Berlin 1997, 1)

Man as a being of intellect wants the entire, absolute knowledge. In the preface to his *Phänomenologie des Geistes* (1807), Hegel (1975) says: "The being is totally mediated", despite the fact that Aristotle already knew the human logos was incapable to completely unify the world (Aristotle, Metaphisics 1006a 5, Ethics Nicomah 1142 a 17sl.). Trends in modern philosophy have been increasingly yielding the totality of knowledge to the subject's organisational-technical ability. Together with the development of science and technology, the subject or the man of modernity has been appropriating the absolute knowledge to completely dominate the world. Because knowledge is the total power, and its guardians prevent it from spreading among the unbidden, as wrote Einstein (Barnett 1950, 9). The absolute knowledge is thus always the competition and struggle for primacy, as is written about Adam and Eve at the beginning of the Bible: "You will not die. For God knows that when you eat of it your eyes will be opened, and you will be like God, knowing good and evil." (Gen 3, 4-5)

Modernity has taken the total thinking to its extremes, in the last centuries it also sees to its applicability – both socio-political and media-procedural.

MacAllister points out: "Totalitarianism arises as an intellectual problem if the differences between Nazism and communism appear cosmetic rather than philosophical" and "… reason became merely instrumental." (McAllister 1995, 36, 46)

Modernity asserts absolute, minutely arranged and systematised knowledge. Its ideal is a modern cybernetic machine, which simultaneously regulates itself (man) and the entire reality: "Our civilisation assumes the structure and characteristics of a machine … and this machine will not settle for less than the total global regime." (Valéry 1962; Gergen 1991, Chapt. 2: *The Metaphor of Machine*)

"And if the imagery of a machine lies at the core of the modernist understanding of a person, then a characteristic of a mature man should be autonomous reliability. A well constructed machine defies limitations (jam, malfunction) and works reliably. In the same way, a mature man will work 'automatically', dependably, trustworthy and constantly, if he is brought up in this manner within his family and by the society." (ibid.)

The modern man has therefore used science and technology to create his cybernetic system, which has in turn absorbed him and assigned him the task to function like a machine.

With the introduction and development of Highlife through modern High-Tech-Phase - aeroplanes, television, media-electronic technology, this machine began to accelerate its functioning and reached the absolute velocity (Virilio, 1977). Modern technical knowledge controls our reality and at frantic speed drives the modern man and his society into the all-against-all struggle, it tries to completely unify this process, which thus politically gained supremacy over man. The excesses of such policy are modern totalitarianisms: "Western liberal democracies suffered from a profound disorder - a sickness unto death - that resulted not from the machinations of our enemies and from the adversities of the human condition but from within ourselves." (McAllister 1996, 64; Lippmann 1955, 5)

Totalitarian absolutisms, as the climax of the modern subject's endeavours to control the reality regardless of means, brought the modern subject itself into subjection to "technical mind". The development of science and technology accelerated post-Enlightenment: "The (new) modern project would no longer rest upon a discredited Semitic cosmology but upon the methods of science." (McAllister 1996, 69) The man of Romanticism as an ideal of completeness and humanity melted into the systemic procedural man. Hence Nietzsche, Husserl and Heidegger criticise modernity for its neglect of humanity. A similar criticism of the modern development came also from existentialists (Jaspers 1951) and the adherents of different movements, especially after the horrors of both World Wars and the Great Depression in the 1930s. In the 1920s, the Youth or Crusaders' movement (R. Guardini) demanded spiritual renovation of Christianity which would serve as the basis for the real renovation of the society. This development makes Eric Voegelin wonder: "What does it mean to be human? What is one's place in the totality of reality?" (McAllister 1996, 75)

"The modern subject surrenders to the procedural process whose consequence is estrangement of spirit. In place of the divine ground of being, man emerges as the ground to himself. The narcissistic closure has many consequences for language and thinking, which today in the socially dominant public of Germany are so evident that there hardly exists anymore a consciousness of their existence", wrote Eric Voegelin

(Voeglin 1971, 12, 21; McAllister 1996, 171). It runs, instead of God, the modern world "with a decapitated metaphysic." (Mc Allister 1996, 175) This is the metaphysics of the technical procedural mind, which became barbarianised: "...and debate is impossible in an intellectually and spiritually balkanized society." (Ibid.)

This barbarization is of course not the result of "Balkan intrigues", it resulted from development of the modern society, which used scientific-technical means to build a modern arsenal of weaponry consolidating and maintaining functionality of a modern state (Virillo 1988). Control of territory allows no dialogue, technology and weapons rule the world and man. Balkan was but one among the exponents of these processes, examples can be found also in Palestine, countries of Africa and Asia, not to forget Afghanistan. During the war in Bosnia and Herzegovina, the bishop Komarica from Banja Luka experienced and obtained from politicians a confirmation of these modern processes. The modern man wants to control the reality by the force of science, technology and weapons. Neo-liberalism again reinforced this trend when it remained the only globalising superpower after the fall of communist systems. Its strength is manifested by globalisation as the world economic-financial process. The leading role in this process is played by the USA which tries to unify the world by its war against terrorism. Its power lies in physical force based on weapons. Globalisation needs corrections. This is confirmed by strong anti-globalist movements which warn the world's superpowers that the might of weapons should be defeated by the power of dialogue, which remains, despite the demanding relationships in the modern world, the only real alternative in solving these problems.

Neo-scholasticism and the Modernity

The Christian Church went through another split at the beginning of modern times (1517). The "East-West schism" (1053) already caused the formation of national Christian churches, which, while retaining the basic foundations of Christian tradition, came closer to national cultures. Despite the common Christian doctrine, the Orthodox Church sociologically acquired, due to national-cultural particularities of individual countries, distinctive national connotations, which formed increasingly firm symbiosis of national-Christian culture, thus tying Christianity to the national trends of modernity. Also because of this, the process of modernity was slowed down within the Orthodox Church, while the Protestant support to national causes was more enlightening-critical, though not preventing the national conditioning of Christianity from its contribution in shaping modern protestant states and their national autonomies. Evangelist Christianity (especially Calvinism) gave an impetus to the industrial-technical development, because *industria* (industry) had theological foundations. The early capitalism also channelled the development of modernity by religious means. Adam Smith thus demanded that capitalists should fear God and should not insatiably crave goods only for themselves, but produce them with moral sentiment for others (Smith 1759 and 1776). After him, Max Weber (1904/5) emphasized that the spirit of Christianity built capitalist society, yet he at the same time realised that this society differentiated and that its subsystems attained independence, which erased the universal religious sense in the society.

God is no longer the foundation of the world order, the system of modernity is slowly but surely beginning to function without Him. Society is no longer governed by Christianity, but by technical-rational mind. Leo Strauss is thus of the opinion (quoted in McAllister, 173): But Nietzsche lived in an age of transition from Christianity to something else, and he wrote *Beyond Good and Evil* as a precursor of the philosopher of the future. Although he was one of those precursors, Nietzsche was nonetheless an heir of Christianity … Because, as Strauss argued, Nietzsche replaced the Platonic Eros and pure mind with will to power. (…) The life-giving creativity of the will to power supplies truths and gods. Nietzsche's natural man is Machiavelli's man, the man of power, the power by which he controls the life of modernity, except in the USA. According to Strauss, however, even the American liberalism after 1950 found itself in crisis and relativism, which means the transition from "firm belief in certain values (i.e. liberal democratic values) to an inability to affirm any values", because the religious foundations, which have so far determined the American society, vanished. We are witnessing the fact that "dogmatic atheism, upon which modern social science rests, erodes the religious beliefs that help make liberal democracy possible - or at least liveable (Ibid., 164). This is today an acute problem not only in the USA, which appeals to "In God we trust", but also in the European and other (liberal) democracies, where the procedural policy of power is becoming increasingly prevalent. The latter is determined by the global capitalist and market-oriented economy, which drives out the weaker. All this is being done systematically through the symbolic establishment of the world, which is shaped by media's decisive "influence on masses". Pre-conscious and subconscious play an important role in this, as stated by important authors. This is the world of scientific-technical projection not the world of man.

How does the Catholic Church respond to these processes of modernity? Is it really about "omnivision of Theos from Judaic-Christian tradition, which gave the impression that we were offered the opportunity to discover the basic structure of being in its totality", as put by Habermas (2001, 175ff.). Does the Church, like other systems of modernity, pursue all-embracing knowledge and control? This process represents a special challenge to the Church because of the increasingly aggressive attempts of the systems of modernity to partially divest the Church of its "omnivision" and drive it to the social margin. This is reflected in the views of popes, particularly those of Benedict XIV and Pius IX, who were at the beginning favourably disposed and open towards the demands of modernity for freedom of thinking and action. Yet they were driven out of the settled socio-political frames (church state, unity of church and state) by violent interventions, so they turned their back on the trends of modernity.

From the sociological perspective, in the unfolding of these developments the Church through Neo-scholasticism took increasingly resolute steps as a parallel system and defied the systems of modernity. Neo-scholasticism, as a total system of thought and control, was by theology gaining deeper foundations, which were the sign of transcending of sociology, but it eventually became, due to external pressures and the need of organisational-technical adjustment, one of the modern systems, although it retained its pre-modern conservative (religious) foundations. This engendered growing discord between the Church and modernity, which is manifested by periods of pronounced crises of the Church in the last two hundred years. These dilemmas appeared most distinctly at the Second Vatican Council. The Church had till then sought a new basis for social, political and cultural action in the world of differentiated and systemically-theoretically organised modernity, but it countered the modern trends with the formally perfected neo-scholastic system. This problem is clearly reflected in the attitudes of popes towards modern trends: the differences in actions of the same popes (Benedict XIV and

Pius IX) and differences in actions of different popes, e.g. the introversion of Pius IX and social openness of Leon XIII), yet the Church always perceives itself as a »perfect society« (*societas perfecta*).

The origin of this process can be traced back in medieval scholasticism, which raised theology to the level of *science (in statum scientiae*), theology thus also provided the foundations for the modern lay scientific-technical image of the world and in turn itself became its competition. Together with science, theology asserted the universal power of rational control over reality and succumbed to delusive glitter of this self-organisation. Under the influence of the most prominent late-scholastic thinker Francis Suarez and other successors of Thomism, the neo-Thomistic universal system, functionally akin to the modern systems of control, emerged from the Thomistic creationistic thought bound up with *potentia oboedientialis creationis*. Within the church institution, this system tried to "develop the basic structure of being in its totality", as put by Habermas (2001, 190); however, it did not accept the modern subjectivity, although it was Christianity that created it.

The processes of modernity and modern differentiation therefore reflect the problem of Christianity which is in this manner organised in different churches. The Catholic (universal) Church found this particularly difficult, because the Church organisationally controlled the world until modern times and spread the religion by missionaries the world over, and with the arrival of modern subjectivities this universal world of the Church fell apart. Through the differences in conceptual or ideological foundations enforced by liberal-national states (France, Italy, Germany, Austria), this image of Christianity experiences escalating conflicts with the forces of modernity. This holds true even for the Austro-Hungarian monarchy, which declared itself as a catholic state, yet departed from Christian values, despite the fact that its emperor hold the title of an apostolic ruler and appointed Catholic bishops. Although his politicians in the Vienna Parliament, for example in 1907 the Slovene Janez Evangelist Krek, spoke in favour of separating the Church from state.

The Church did not accept subjective points of departure of Hermes, Günther or Baader, characterising them as semi-rationalism (DS 2914, 2919). On one hand, these thinkers build on the subject's openness in faith, yet they do not advocate complete rationalism. On the other hand, they are condemned by the Church exactly for their enforcing of modern subjective (semi)rationalism. The neo-scholastic system thus strengthens the functionality of faith and the Church in contrast to modernity, whose trends jeopardize the Church. Trends of modernity - variants of liberalism in particular, are more and more energetically opposing this by the basic modern weapon – by subjectivity, which is within the Church covered by neo-scholastic totality. The Church for this reason tries to secure an indisputable and complete theological view of the world (*omnivisio*), which should a priori enable it on theological bases to be competitive with the systems of modernity. Neo-scholasticism, instead of becoming *potentia oboedientialis* (Thomas Aquinas, S. Th. III, q. 11 a.1c; *De veritate* q. 29 a. 3) and freedom of the believing, thus becomes the pitfall of its absolute formation of objective knowledge and the pertaining control of the world. The systems of modernity (science: Galilei; politics: Machiavelli, Hobbes; society: Marx) divest the Church of its legitimacy based precisely on these points, which are not immanent to the Church, since it admitted the "autonomy of earthly realities" on the Second Vatican Council, (GS Nr. 36), which is relative (in faith) with regard to God (Ibid. 36/3), yet autonomous in regard to the Earth.

In order to secure its mobility within the world of modernity, the Church therefore tried, on the basis of its set social extension and conditioning, to compete with the "neo-scholastic omnivisio", which is systemically-functionally more mobile and technically-rationally more elaborate and organised system of modernity. However, the organisational form could not mediate the appropriate new contents. Besides this, the circular letter *Aeterni Patris* 4. Aug. 1879 by Leon XIII refers to Thomas Aquinas, who set the best foundations of theology and is thus "granted the most distinguished placed (priority) within the Church." (DS 3139, 3140) Yet neo-scholasticism failed to pay due attention to Thomas' maintenance of the tension between the faith and the rational system, which is clearly manifested by the event from 1273, the so-called revelation of Aquinas: "All I have written is trash if compared to what I saw and what was revealed to me." (Torell 1995, 302)

The Church, as a pre-modern system, organised in a modern way with a hierarchical symbolism (Virillo 1988), its power rests on emphasising that the earthly reality depends on God, for which only faith is competent, not the intellect; so the Church can compete with modern systems only by faith. This is confirmed also by the exposé of John XXIII and in particular by the Second Vatican Council, as well as by the exposés of the pope John Paul II – especially his constant advocating of dialogue and non-violence in modern world. This is a model the Church can apply in modernity; when it advocates the foundation of faith, it acts in accord with the demands of modernity.

Church and society: a post-modern vision and vision of faith

Pier Aldo Rovatti says that J. Vattimo, who resumes the criticism of domineering thinking of modernity (as put forward by Nietzsche, Husserl and Heidegger), advocates the so-called "weak thinking."(Vattimo 1997, 27) Regardless of the arguable timing of the criticism addressed to the "weak thinking", we can agree with Vattimo that the problem of the domineering knowledge of modernity lies in its suppression of the subject's integrity, despite the fact that this modernity triggered his autonomy in the first place. Modern systems tend towards operability and total control of reality; in the opinion of Paul Virillo (1977) and Jean Baudrillard (2010) the system runs more and more quickly, so man can no longer control it with his intellect – he who created the system fell prey to the system's control, the system which is now determined by the liberal economy with its consumerism and media. It would be also interesting to explore the role which Christian churches played in establishing and maintaining communist systems that gained ground primarily in the societies with a tradition of obedience, which was conditioned also by consolidating of the society's economic patterns (Russia, China, as well as some Catholic countries - Poland, Slovenia, Spain). It is interesting that Marxism was not established, according to the expectations and predictions of its theoreticians, in the societies with a distinctively modern (protestant) autonomist tradition.

Vattim believes that the "weak thinking" prevailed primarily due to philosophy as well as Christianity because it took part in shaping modernity. Vattimo defines the "weak thinking" in contrast to total thinking as thinking which includes not only the history of being, but also the history of its weaknesses and nihilism. Vattimo thinks that we can only in this way avoid, in a Heideggerian sense, the totally domineering thinking and its total nihilism. The "weak thinking" is the thinking of man, a person: his ability to govern his situation, yet at the same time the ability to take into account his own dependency, pitfalls and mistakes, and thus also recognising his own limitations and temporalness (Heidegger). Here, according to Vattimo, is where philosophy and

Christianity meet or complement, accepting such thinking is therefore the obligation of all institutions: state and civil, also the Church. The conditions for establishing such thinking are:

(1) Respecting the integral image of man (integer) or man's autonomy as a person; (2) This in turn forms the basis of the subsidiary society; (3) Taking into account the transcendence of a person; (4) Interpersonal solidarity; and (5) Dialogue.

(1) In his essay *Beantwortung der Frage: Was ist die Aufklärung*: *Sapere aude*, Kant (1964, 53ff.) demands the following: Have courage to use your mind. To educate people to become mature, independent and responsible persons means to allow for man's personal autonomy. The Christian social teaching is based on man as a person in the likeness of Jesus Christ, which is written in the documents of the Second Vatican Council (GS Nr. 12sl., 22) and in circular letters of the last popes. In view of the omnipresent manipulation, the enslavement of man by media and others, it is even more important today, as put by Leonardo Boff, that man can be wilfully present everywhere. We need autonomous people who do not succumb to opinions, prejudices or merely external commands. This requires that the Church also within itself educate autonomous, mature and independent persons – Christians who can be the salt of the earth and ready to defy these traps and challenges of the modern world. Prophetic attitude can be based only on such mature and independent person. As early as in the middle of the 20th century, Karl Jaspers pointed out that amidst modern technology man needs to regain his face, which is a prerequisite for the successful future of human society (Jaspers 1951).

(2) The principle of subsidiarity is based on the Christian social order (circular letter QA 1931, Nr. 86-88), which became the foundation of the world's democratic order. This principle takes into account the direct competence of a person and persons, for they themselves will best evaluate a situation and act accordingly. A society which is founded from below secures its successful development. Modernity stuck in a cul-de-sac precisely because of the total systems regulated from above. Though they started from autonomy of a person, both liberalism and neo-liberalism neglected this principle, which is a problem of modern democracy. Local or regional competent self-government is the basis of a successful society. Ulrich Beck says that today we must act globally by acting locally (locally - globalisation is glocalisation; Beck 2000, 238).

The locus is thus of utmost importance. Only subsidiary society can be a democratic society which enforces particularistic justice (Michael Walzer). Globalisation uses media to turn the world into a single village (McLuhan: Global Village), this village should be allowed self-regulation (from below). The Church accepted the sodality principle, but the institution now faces problems caused by the aforementioned development of the Church's structure which is modelled after modernity. The prospects and future of the Church lay in its local autonomy, which will obligate the lower to settle their own affairs in faith.

(3) Modernity created a one-sided image of man as a person. Science, technology and media-treatment of life subjected man's image to become robot-like, perfect and absolute. Jobs demand more and more accomplished people who function one hundred percent. Because man as a rule falls short of this ideal, the number of depressive people is increasing, in some places even to 45% of all population. The research has shown that the constant fluctuation due to inability to reach the norms brings about new problems, namely, co-workers constantly have to adapt to each other. Man is as a person indeterminable, exceeding being; to put it in a Christian way: people are beings open to God. No one can nor should appropriate us completely. The integrity of a person is thus assured in God. The person's foundation in God in turn assures his autonomy, enabling him to overcome his limitations, to resist evil, and, since he knows his own limitations, to be tolerant towards his fellowmen. Politicians, public officials and priests will be able to act independently and justly if they internalise deeper motives (in faith). Within the Church, the foundation of a person in God is the basic condition and driving force of the Church's work, it is its specificity in the world. Everything has its standards, its organisation and its entire sense only in faith. This is an eminent task performed by Christians and the Church community on the Earth. All else derives meaning from this. Even the operating of state institutions and civil society is incomplete and lacks the appropriately deep basis, which provides dependable regulation of interpersonal problems, if they do not admit that man as a person exceeds any system.

(4) The foundation in faith qualifies persons also for solidarity. Globalisation integrates economically, media display undreamed-of possibilities, yet we need universal solidarity which will enable man to satisfy at least his minimal needs. This begins again on the local level. The question »Who is my fellowman« is answered in close proximity to

each other, people can be overlooked if viewed from afar. Solidarity means openness towards others, which are beings of need. Man in distress needs his fellowmen – this is the key for solving problems of the modern world. If economists, financiers and politicians do not feel solidarity, they will still build a functional society, but they will also bring about their own slow demise in the same society. Man is today lonely also in the Church, especially a priest, who is on the margin of the hierarchical system, a solitary defender of faith in the company of modernity. The need for associating is also confirmed by the movements which unite people within the Church into the community - into *ecclesia*.

(5) The solution of complicated problems of the modern world and the Church is conditional also on dialogue, to which all other enumerated conditions point. Church documents call attention to dialogue (e.g. GS Nr. 1, 2, 58, 82; Paul VI, *Ecclesiam suam* 1964 et al.); it is pointed out by post-modern thinkers; politicians shoot their mouth about it. Every war, too, has to end in dialogue. Man comes into the world and is able to survive only in dialogue (with mother and other people). Dialogue is the basic form of human interaction. Man's symbolic world is established through dialogue. Dialogue is the fundamental frame of the Church's work (Paul VI). The Church can and should set an example of dialogic solutions of problems. Dialogistic predisposition also makes us open to God. Jesus comes to the world to tell us about the Father, retreats from the world to enable the Holy Spirit to act through him. Dialogue within the Church opens us to the Spirit: the Church acts through it when it testifies in faith. The world of today is due to strained relations forced into dialogue. Dialogue in politics, economy and elsewhere is a precondition for survival. Anti-globalist demonstrations and sophisticated questions of integration demand dialogic disposition, because this is the only hope for the future of mankind. The spreading of technology and media opposes this principle, yet man has no other choice. Family, in particular, should educate for dialogue, although today this may prove a difficult task. Dialogically firm and associated persons feel together and are stronger when it comes to solving their problems or helping others. For the Christians within the Church, such alliance today represents almost the matter of survival of the faith and the Church, it is thus the key issue of relating among ourselves and with others. The necessity for dialogue between religions is also becoming more and more apparent. It is not so much about a single world ethos (H. Küng) as about

strengthening one's own ethos by enriching it with other religions. The depth of faith provides firmness and openness towards others, since profundity is the place where people of different religions and beliefs can meet. That is why Gandhi said what is now repeated by Dalai Lama - we do not need convert to other religions, but deepen our own. Deeply religious and socially sensitive persons will be capable of empathy and co-existence with the different (*sympáthos*). It is thus possible to overcome, in the sense of the post-modern demand which is, according to Habermas, "the most creative part of philosophic reflection", also the present conflicts: the problems of male and female equity (Benhabib), false and genuine identity (M. Foucault, R. Rorty, Horster 1999, 101), disappearance of reality (Baudrillard/Guattari), the problem of equity among discourses (Lyotard), as well as to preserve the other as the other and different (Levinas 1987, 44).

2. AUTONOMOUS PERSON AS THE BASIS OF ETHICS - MAN BETWEEN MODERN AND POSTMODERN MORALITY

Man as the basis or a "starting point"

The man as an autonomous human being is the basis of ethics. Man is the being of acts. If he is acting, he is realizing himself as the being within free will. The free will is, as Kant (1956/1788, A4ff.) stressed, the basis of ethics. Man is naturally disposed to act according to his free will, thus also within ethics. Yet the acting man is involved in various relations. They determine his free will and the circumstances of his person, his character, his will and the position of good. This produces different observations about the role of man's free will in his life.

The Aristotelian and Aquinas' view was that man as a natural being is also the source of ethics (gr. *ethos*). Aquinas related it to man's natural aspirations to the good. The ultimate good is God (Akvinski, 1999: 307: *Summa contra gentiles* I. 2, cap 47-48; *Quaestiones disputatae de malo*, q. 6). As such, man is also the basis of himself, because through his acts he is coming to himself, as Fichte (1965) pointed out.

The Stoics emphasized the ethical role of man in the society and environment as such. The person (gr. *prósopon*, lat. *persóna*) has according to Cicero (106-43), who took these ideas from the Stoic philosopher Panaitios (180-110), four roles. The first one is intellect. The second is the type of construction or the character of man. Then there are two more societally and personally conditioned types of man. The third one is environment, surroundings of man; the forth role is the man's choice, his occupation (Cicero 1975, 107-125).

Arthur Schopenhauer adds that man's ethical acting depends on his character. Man cannot act completely freely, he will act according to his character (Schopenhauer 1991, 449). It means that the source of ethics is man as a being in his totality, not only his pure will, not an isolated, pure self, but the self within its personal and social relations, as Taylor would say.

Rainer Marten (Marten 2000, 98) also emphasises that the verity of "humanum" is practical. Man truly becomes man through his actions. This includes his environmental, interpersonal and personal relations, which is a practical matter. The successful emotional relationships are the most important aspect of this practical side. These are based on successful interpersonal relationships, especially in the first years of man's life: "For side by side with conceptual language there is an emotional language; side by side with logical or scientific language there is a language of poetic imagination. Primarily language does not express thoughts or ideas, but feelings and affections." (Cassirer 1974, 25)

Personality of Man

The picture of man in the European tradition was influenced mostly by Christianity. Man is the image of God and God is the basis of the personality and integrity of man. The Christians pointed out that the person of Jesus Christ was the basis of this personality. Man is thus the image of God (*imago Dei*). All his relations are entirely founded in God. This presupposes that (human) nature is of divine character. As Boethius (480-525 or 526) said, the personality has a man, God and an angel (Boethius 1999, 85). Man and God have the personality (Boethius, 1999, 95), they have the same basis, its self-consciousness. Yet God is giving the nature of man, especially his spiritual nature.

The Augustinian God is also nature: *Deus est natura scilicet non creata, sed creatrix*: God is nature, which means it is not created but the creator (Augustin 1975, 1057). Because God is the Creator, he is the source of (human) nature, the source of all. God provides the basis of man. If man will provide for himself through his nature, he has to observe the will of God. The source of man is the source of God, because God is the interior of man.

Man and God could not be separated from one another. Even more - God is the basis of man's acting, thus of his moral conduct.

Aquinas (1224-1274) pointed out that the nature is autonomous and man has to observe this natural order (Akvinski 1999, 563). If man observes the natural order, he engages his will in the order of natural development to the final goal – the good in God. This is not against the will of man, on the contrary – if he observes the order of the world, he is perfecting himself and the world.

According to Aristotle, man has the same position as animals because he has a body. The body makes man dependent, since he could not expresses himself without a body (Gilson 1984). He also depends on his corporality to perform this task. Unlike animals, man can control his body, because he can remember (Aristoteles 1999 - 1st book 980b25-28). He enables himself to use his body, to receive perceptions, to sort them out, to transform them into ideas and to establish them as habits (gr. *éthos*), thus organizing himself within his environment. Man needs to organise himself in order to live. He anticipates future and foresees (gr. *phrónesis*) his life (Prometheus). He develops the ability to foresee and to act in accordance with his foresight. He plans ahead his own life.

Dependence and independence

Acting so, he is in a way independent, because he controls the conditions of his life. Yet he depends on his corporality, he is entangled in natural and social circumstances to perform this task, and the ultimate responsibility for this is with him. In this vein MacIntyre concludes that there are two virtues enabling man to conduct a good life – the first is his practical intellect guiding him to independence. The other lies in the acknowledgement of his innate dependence (MacIntyre 1999). Here man faces the permanent danger of being oppressed by systems.

The dialectics between dependence and independence lies in the man's fundamental capacity to be the body and mind, to be the being of language and dialogue. Man is thus, as Gordon Allport pointed out, a basis and a cause of the society: "How can the individual be both a cause and a consequence of society?" (Allport 1968, 9) We can add: how can he be a basis and a cause of the self. The dialogue (the language) combines man's independence and his dependence from others and from nature. The language enables man to compensate his physical inferiority in relation to animals and to subdue nature to create his own world.

As a child, man needs mother who enables him to survive. He comes into this world completely dependent. The dialogue with mother enables the child to enter the human community. "Hence, there must be a bidirectional relation between maternal personality and child personality … Bowlby (1969/1982) claims that humans have an innate need for social interaction that becomes focused on the specific figure over the course of the first year of life. This attachment to a specific figure (or figures) has evolutionary significance in that it has survival value for the species." (Eder; Mangelsdorf 1997, 211) "In sum, during infancy, early affective experience forms the basis for the child's developing self-concept." (Eder; Mangelsdorf 1997, 220) This means the whole personality, his relations to the social and natural world in their totality: the personality is based on this early experience of a human being with his/her parents and other relational persons.

Through mother the child will be enabled to communicate in the symbolic forms of human behaviour, to participate in the human society and to overcome nature. The examples of the children who were brought up by animals show us that man can not survive as such if he cannot share the first years of his life with the human community. A child must be taught by the others (the community), otherwise he/she cannot develop his/her symbolic capacities. Man's ability to survive can be developed only through the dialogue between human beings.

Man needs other people, through dialogue man develops the ability to govern himself, his body and nature. To be precise – he develops the ability to govern himself and the world through other persons. On one side he learns to be independent from others, on the other side he tries to be connected with other people. Human nature is thus not based on an individual person but on the mankind as such: "Culture and social structure impinge on individuals through their subjective interpretation. A major social psychological contribution on this area is its insistence that the linkages between personality and social structure must involve processes that include the individual's perceptions of the social environment." (Pettigrew 1997, 432)

Poor conditions (circumstances) for interpersonal relations are the problem of our time. A young person cannot develop the capacities for interpersonal relationships. She/he cannot develop the emotional basis of a person which would enable her/him to get into a contact with other person. It is very difficult to correct this conditioning later, because in the first three years of our lives we get the basic codes which set the manner and the basis of our interaction with the world. "We believe that the common thread between early personality development and later adult personality lies in individual differences in emotionality." (Eder; Mangelsdorf 1997, 209) In this development lies the answer to the question of human ethics. The ability for the ethical acting is conditioned through the child's early emotional experience. Man has the primordial hereditary ability for moral acting. Yet this ability can be developed only through other people. Two sources combine to produce this ethical ability – the first is the philosophical or ontological, the second is psychological.

The ontological basis of ethics – Modern concepts of ethics?

We have seen the importance which the psychological background has for man's ethical ability. The crucial questions here are: what kind of relation exists between psychological and ontological background, what is the ethical basis of a person? In other words – what is the guarantee that a person has enough ethical power to act ethically. Let us consider some views of modern[1] philosophy on this question and then to come to the postmodern views.

Neoscholasticism

The first one is the scholastical, or neoscholastical, to be accurate. The scholastics defend the unity of being, truth, goodness and beauty. The scholastics derived from a being a priori goodness as the possibility of a good action. If the being is good, good actions will follow. "Der Ursprung der Unbedingtheit sittlicher Werte liegt in der Faktizität des idealen Seins." (Schiller 1993, XXIV) The ideal order is the order of good, and man as a being in the high sense is capable to establish this order: "Human beings differ from irrational creatures in this, that they have dominion over their actions. That is why only those actions over which a human being has dominion are called human. But it is thanks to reason and will that human beings have dominion over their acts: free will *(liberum arbitrium)* is said to be the faculty of reason and will." (Aquinas STh I. II. Q.1 a.1 - McInerny 1995, 197) There is another reason that man's morality possesses some ultimate truth, it is natural law: "The set of the principles of moral discourse is what Aquinas means by natural law." (McInerny 1995, 210) But there are not only moral principles. The man has a capability – an inclination to pursuit them: man has an inclination towards good. Aquinas was also a theologian, and he taught that man is corrupted by the original sin, so he does not always follow the good. Through faith man can reach his moral goal and perfect himself: "At the top of the hierarchy of laws is the *eternal law,* which he defines as 'the rational governance of everything on the part of God as a

1 "Modern" means in the time of modernity, it is the time of low and high tech equipments and the time of the modern systems. (Gergen 1996)

ruler of the universe' (STh I. II. q.91 a.1) and identifies as divine providence. *Natural law*, ranked below the eternal law, is defined by Aquinas as 'the participation in the eternal law by rational creatures'." This participation is performed through "a natural inclination to their proper action and ends." (STh I. II. q. 91 a.2 - Sigmund 1995, 223) Without faith, man cannot easily reach the perfection and fulfil his aims. This means that man can do good deeds in his life also without faith. The system alone cannot enable him to reach the ultimate goals of his life.

Neoscholastics tried to make from Aquinas' moral philosophy the system of morality. They perfected the moral system as an ideally grounded system. It does not surprise that the Slovenian philosopher Anton Mahnič (1850-1920) contends (1912) that morality has a metaphysical constellation. It enables a solid background for ethical acting. If the world is ontologically grounded and the being is true, good and beautiful, than the moral acting has ontological status. Man is grounded in it. Mahnič called it Platonian trinity of the ontological realities: truth, goodness and beauty. It is self-evident that man can perform good actions, because he is based on it. There is also the equivalence of a person and good, because they are both based on the universal unity of being. The guarantee of this unity is God as an ontological source of all beings. Because of this ontological relation between being and good, man is in principle able to perform good deeds. If he does otherwise, this has not internal but external causes; this means that something happened which prevented his good deeds.

The neoscholastic view of morality is a typical (systematic) modern view of morality. According to Alasdair MacIntyre, however, the neoscholastics made the rapture between the heritage of Aquinas and modern philosophy (MacIntyre 2003, 59). The epistemological question was thus the main question of neoscholasticism: "Yet those who responded to *Aeterni Patris* all too often followed Kleutgen in making epistemological concerns central to Thomism." (MacIntyre 2003, 75) The system is well grounded if man is in harmony with it, if he performs his moral task. If not, we should find the reason for his unlucky ways. It can be found quickly – the man was not obeying or following the system. He strayed from the real ontological source of the morality and did not accept the entire moral framework.

France Veber

The Slovenian philosopher France Veber (1890-1975) used the Aristotelian background (with a modern starting-point) to develop his phenomenological theory of object with his graduations of different objects of consciousness. The consciousness is not only the psychological but also the real basis of the unity of being. Even more – this unity combines all abilities of a person to reach metaphysics or Gegenstandstheorie (Theory of Objects - Veber 1921, 70-71). What does this mean? The objects or objectives are the "facts of consciousness". The consciousness makes the unit of (logical) system of all objects and thus also the objects of ethics: "My ethics, which is presented in this text, aspire to be no less or more than the particular logic, so far unknown within this systematics, that is the logic of emotions and strivings – the logic of the heart." (Veber 1923, 7)

How can this scientific ethics be reached? The ethical sphere is a part of the total domain of the object world. The object world of the consciousness is divided into four classes of experiences: notions, thoughts, emotions and strivings (Veber 1921, 99). These experiences give rise to four series of objects: foundations, facts, values and "oughtnesses." (Veber 1921, 305)

It should be noted that Veber distinguishes between psychological and apsychological validity of objects. He is convinced that with the apsychological validity of objects the scientific status of the ethics can be reached. Initially, objects have psychological status, but through scientific analysis they acquire apsychological validity. It means that all objects have logical status, they are logically proved. Man has the ability to prove and confirm this logical status of objects. Thus the scientific system of ethics is established. The system of ethics is according to Veber only one among the derivations of the theory of objects.

This Veberian ethics of values is ethics *more geometrico*. Values are in the consciousness objectively confirmed and are thus the real object of striving, the "oughtnesses". Veber was quite certain that the ethical system has a universal validity regardless of whether the participants recognise it or not. The system works in itself. In this way Veber called himself a moral apriorist, like Kant. Yet he distinguished himself from Kant – in his own words – by being a consecutive apriorist, while he considered Kant a constitutive apriorist. It is clear that Veber based his ethics on Christianity, and he presupposed fundamental faith in the positive meaning of reality. In this way he could be sure about the apsychological reality of objects, including the objects of striving for the "oughtnesses". The Christian heritage enabled the firmness of the moral system.

Alasdair MacIntyre

No modern theory of ethics can neglect the contribution to the discussion on this matter by Alasdair MacIntyre. His moral philosophy is based on the historical and contemporary experiences of morality: "He has been also influenced, in ways that are unusual for most Anglophone moral philosophers, by thought of such continental figures as Gadamer, Maritain, and, more recently, Edith Stein and Husserl." (Solomon 2003, 114) His work *After Virtue* (1981) is based on the traditional Aristotelian-Scholastic heritage of the good. He also recognises the relation between human nature and the ability of a person to fulfil his moral obligation. Yet he also places the moral philosophy in the context of historical development and in the sociological context. He went through various important moral standpoints and worked out the concept that modern moral philosophers emphasized a partial view of the ethical tradition. MacIntyre is on one side a philosopher of modernity, while on the other he is critical towards the majority of modern solutions, especially in ethics. He blames the enlightenment philosophy for the desolateness of the stage of moral thought, for "the incoherent conceptual scheme which we have inherited." (MacIntyre 1986, 68)

He is criticising the intuitionism of the Utilitarians, especially of Moore: "Emotivism thus understood turns out to be as a cogent theory of use rather than a false theory of meaning, connected with one specific stage in moral development or decline, a stage which our own culture entered early in the present century." (MacIntyre 1986,18)

The sin of modern moral philosophy originates with Kant, because he rejected the philosophy of values and reduced all morality to normative ethics, to the moral imperative. The same source of the protestant heritage is the problem of Kierkegaard's ethics (MacIntyre 1986, 44). They both built their ethics on the protestant tradition and so they do not need to ground their ethics on values, instead they trust intuitionism and emotivism (MacIntyre 1986, 45). The same critique applies to the Veberian position of ethics.

MacIntyre believes that Kant and Kierkegaard neglected the important ethical heritage of Aristotle and Aquinas. Preserving and stressing the meaning of the holistic ethical tradition is important also for the correct anthropological view of man in the moral philosophy: "It will be necessary, that is to write a short history of conceptions of the virtues in which Aristotle provides a central point of focus, but which yield the resources of a whole tradition of acting which Aristotle's is only a part, a tradition of which I spoke earlier as 'the classical tradition' and whose of view of man I called 'the classical view of man'." (MacIntyre 1986, 112)

MacIntyre is on one hand seen as an anti-theorist, as an unsystematic philosopher, because he is critical of every philosopher, but on the other hand "…his strong commitment to moral realism (Aristotle, r. J.J.) and his rejection of postmodern perspectivist and relativist views put him at odds with many characterized" in this way…" (Solomon 1986, 131) In his critique of a liberal society he points out that mere procedure is not enough, it should be based on the ability of a person to behave morally. The norms are not enough to preserve the moral ability in the society. It needs virtues. "A virtue is an acquired human quality the possession and exercise of which tends to enable us to achieve those goods which are internal to practices and the lack of which effectively prevents us from achieving any such goods." (MacIntyre 1986, 191) MacIntyre sees the possibility to include virtues if the societal conditions are prepared. The institutions must function well, the technical skills should be adopted and the discussions about the relations among all this devices should take place (MacIntyre 1986, 193). He emphasises the role of a community, but he also takes into account the role of an individual. The psychological research (Winnicot and others) shows us that a child needs support of parents, while for the development of his self-consciousness he also needs the exercise of autonomy to accept the reality of life (MacIntyre 2001, 100).

MacIntyre is a very controversial philosopher (Solomon 2003). He has built his moral system on the Aristotelian-Scholastic tradition. He has stressed the important influence of the culture and sociology on the moral concepts of man. He was trying to solve man's apories – quandaries in the modern world. He stressed the importance of virtues which enable man to work and function in this world. He demanded the support of sciences and institutions. He criticised the Nietzschean irrationalism because it "defies reason", yet "remains immanent in Weberian managerial forms of our culture." (MacIntyre 1986, 115)

MacIntyre criticises the modern "social landscape", such as the philosophy of Nietzsche and the sociology of Weber and Goffman. The question remains: how will MacIntyre overcome the problems of postmodern man, who cannot enable himself to live with virtues. MacIntyre is right when he says this is a consequence of our world's development. He is right when he says that man should be trained in virtues, though modern man is not able to accept this yoke. With his insistence on the system of order, MacIntyre is on the border between modern and postmodern world. In his evaluation of MacIntyre's philosophy, J.L.A. Garcia says that "justice and moral reasoning depend upon fairly specific standards of application and, because of that, also depend on social group." (Murphy 2003, 103) MacIntyre emphasizes man's cultural and ontological ground, while Taylor favours much more the anthropological side of man.

Charles Taylor

Postmodern wo/man has to point out the relation between his own nature and the *nomos* in order to fulfil his moral obligation. The modern *nomos* seems to be devoid of its ethical contents. It is merely the procedural obligation. As the discussion between liberalists and philosophers of good shows, the problem lies in the real position of good. While some liberal philosophers (Rawls 1993 and others) try to show that man is bound to maintain the ethical obligation, philosophers of good, e.g. Taylor, emphasize the necessity for the contents of good in man's life. But what is the basis of this good? As Fukuyama put it – how can we get "ethical capital"? (Fukuyama 2000) Is the good of an individual grounded as the good of the (entire) society? Is it possible to find some ethical saints? And finally – could something like virtues be confirmed in human nature, and how can we get this?

Man as a problem per se and the society

The Kantian view of man regards man as a free being. His freedom is the reason for his morality. Freedom can be recognized because man is acting like a moral being. How and why could Kant (1956/1788: V) pose this assertion? Why can we suppose that man is the source of ethical actions?

The Kantian view of things presupposes that only man's rational nature is the reason of a moral action. It is in accordance with the modern view of man as a person. Modern biologists argue that there are no reasons to say that man is a person because of his rational nature (Schmücker/Steinvorth 2002, 143; Merkel 2002, 156). Today this dilemma can be seen as the question about ethical sources of the society, the question MacIntyre still asks.

In former times (in the classical age of Greece and in the Middle Ages) man's ethical status was enabled by the society. It was hierarchically structured and did not pay any special attention to an individual, as Taylor points out: "The original idealization of this order of mutual benefit comes in a theory of rights and of legitimate rule. It starts with individuals and conceives the society as established for their sake. Political society is seen as an instrument for something prepolitical. The individualism signifies a rejection of the previously dominant notion of hierarchy, according to which a human being can be a proper moral agent only when embedded in a larger social whole, whose very nature is to exhibit a hierarchical complementarity." (Taylor 2004, 19)

Man as a culturally based being

Man's freedom is his constitutional element. With other words – man's free will is the ground of the ethical: "Ethisch gibt es nur den einen Wert, das Gutsein des Willens in vollkommener Abwendung vor aller Selbstsucht. In einer Welt ohne Menschen und in einer ewig vollkommenen Welt gibt es nichts mehr zu fordern, zu idealisieren und zu bessern." (Schiller 1993, XXX) Man is because of this, as we have seen, a symbolic being (Cassirer 1974). He symbolizes the world and he can reach the reality only with symbolical devices. He does not do anything which is not accepted by his symbolical ability. His existence is, as Karl Jaspers pointed out, "a possible existence or existence transcending itself, so that it cannot be the 'object' of anybody's science." (Jaspers 1962, 138) Man is ungraspable; he cannot be described in scientific terms. The ancient Greeks understood the language as an activity, as the condition for all others activities (Kamlah 1973, 43).

This can be observed particularly in the first years of man's life. The child can speak only through other people. He comes to himself through the other. Taylor says: "Human beings are self-interpreting animals." (Taylor 1985, 45) Walter Schaupp, an interpreter of Taylor, points out that according to Taylor man is "subject of systems of sense, meaning, symbols." (Schaupp 2003, 154)

The speaking of "self" is symbolic, too. This is the reason why different meanings appear within the 'self', especially in modern philosophy. In general, modern philosophy tried to neutralise the 'self'. Modern philosophy is thus characterized as a 'disengagement' philosophy. It is a philosophy which bereaves the subject "of all its relations or relationships." (Schaupp 2003, 164) The entire modern philosophy since Descartes suffers from isolations of the self. But the self is no abstract entity, it is the union of different relations, elements and shapes. That is stressed also by MacIntyre.

Disengagement

The main thesis of Taylor's moral philosophy is that the subject is involved in different relations. He is therefore criticizing the views of Descartes and Locke. Taylor labelled Descartes' position as "neutralisation of the world. "The Lockean subject is in this respect quite new. He is essentially non of his properties. What defines him is the abstract power to remake these properties … What does essentially define him is self-consciousness." (Taylor 1989, 615) The problem is that this subjective consciousness is made of points, it is isolated and abstract. It is the problem of the entire modern philosophy. Taylor pointed out that moral thinking is influenced by the radical changes towards subjectivity: "It is a culture which is individualist in the three senses I invoked earlier: it prizes autonomy; it gives an important place to self-exploration, in particular of feeling; and its visions of the good life generally involve personal commitment. As a consequence, in its political language, it formulates the immunities due people in terms of subjective rights. Because of its egalitarian bent, it conceives the rights as universal." (Taylor 1995, 305)

Universalism is the form of egalitarian individualism. It means that all subjects are compelled to do good. But it is only an exterior bind. The modern social theory is atomism and instrumentalism. This is followed by the modern idea of natural and neutral science: "The ideal of disengagement defines a certain – typically modern – notion of freedom, as the ability to act on one's own, without outside interference or subordination to outside authority." (Taylor 1985, 4) The consequence of this isolation of modern man is his inclination to control and subordination. The modern imperial system tries to get this isolated wo/man and to subjugate him.

"All this is answer to the question why it is necessary to belabour the obvious fact that qualitative distinctions have an inexpungable place in our moral life and thinking. We have to fight uphill to rediscover the obvious, to counteract the layers of suppression of modern moral consciousness. It is a difficult thing to do. But what is the point of doing it? In a way, this is to ask: What is the point of articulacy about the good? We tend to have a prejudice in favour of articulacy in our culture (at least in the academy), and so the question may not seem to need an answer. But in fact there have been cogent reasons put forward, or at least hinted at, for a saving inarticulacy in this domain. Some things perhaps ought to be passed over in silence. Ludwig Wittgenstein, among others certainly thought so." (Taylor 1996, 90f.)

What is really the source of morality? Taylor asked this question and he went through the entire modern thinking about morality. He concludes that moral thinking in modern times was dragged into the dungeon of the subject. He speaks about the "critic of naturalism from a hermeneutical standpoint." (Taylor 1985, 4) However, it is very important for Taylor, like for MacIntyre, that this self-interpretation has a dialectical – hermeneutical structure.

The dialectical self as a balance of morality – Taylor's concept of morality

The man is a self-interpreting being: "Through all this cross-talk about "'hermeneutics'", the question of what one means by this basic thesis, that man is a self-interpreting-animal, and how one can show that it is so may still go unanswered." (Taylor 1985, 45) Man is acting in a situation and he is giving his action the meaning which depends on goals of his actions. "But then we must speak of man as a self-interpreting being, because this kind of interpretation is not an optional extra, but is an essential part of our existence. For our feelings always incorporate certain articulations; while just because they do so they open us up on to a domain of imports which call for further articulation. The attempt to articulate further is potentially a life-time process." (Taylor 1985, 65)

Emotions have a very important role in this processes, this will be made clear through language: "Thus because our subject-referring import-attributing emotions are shaped by the way we see the imports. And the way we see the imports is shaped by the language we come to be able to deploy, language shapes these emotions." (Taylor 1985, 72)

The freedom of man derives from thus situated self. The pure freedom is nonsense, because the freedom of man is always conditioned by his relations to the world. "Full freedom would be situationless. And by the same token it would be empty. Complete freedom would be a void in which nothing would be worth doing, nothing would deserve to count for anything." (Taylor 1979, 64)

Taylor is working out a hermeneutical concept of man and his freedom. It is an anthropologically articulated reason – the reason with relations: "Practical reasoning … is a reasoning in transitions. It aims to establish, not that some position is correct absolutely, but rather that some position is superior to some other." (Taylor 1996, 72) "The descriptions given (a) must check out the best means of validation recognized at that time for descriptions of their type (b) they must be consistently applied." (Taylor 1995, 157)

It is very important to obtain consistent theories. And they should be obtained by the interdialogical exchange of moral experiences. The progress of history is not always positive like in Hegel; the man has to weigh and balance between authentic goods and truths on one hand, and among an error-reducing-move on the other. Schaupp says: "Resumed unfolds Taylor the concept of reason which corresponds to the anthropological facets of an engaged self." (Schaupp 2003, 286) But man's ability is to reason and to interpret the circumstances and the grounds of the intercultural and interpersonal goods. So man can enable himself in hermeneutical thinking. The most important ability in this case is for man to express his emotions in the language. This depends on his educational and cultural background. If man is apt to see these conditions, he will live his life authentically and also ethically.

Summary of Taylor's concepts

Taylor is adherent of the evolutionary thinking which facilitates man's possibilities in life:

- He is criticising Hegel's optimistic view of man's and society's development. He corrects Hegel and he not only takes into account man's individual development, but also stresses the development of a society on the socio-cultural level. Only by the way of the "comparativist enterprise" can the ethical man "give people of every culture some sense of the immense gamut of human potentialities" (Taylor 1997, 164) to enable religions and civilisations to cooperate and overcome the clashes.
- His concept of good is transformed also through Heidegger's analysis of existence. Man can develop good in himself if he is not an isolated self but open to different possibilities of his being. These are biographical-individual and historical-cultural. Inspired by Gadamer, he points out the "meaning event" and the sense of life. He stresses the meaning of emotions in man's life. The meaning event is an emotional awareness. It presupposes a dynamic subject who is involved in an existential situation.
- The third point of Taylor's analysis of good as a basis of moral subjects is his linguistic-theoretical basis. Good is communicable, it should be discussed and shared by the whole competent language-community. Taylor is here inspired by Wittgenstein's "ordinary language".
- The good in man is determined by sensuousness and thinking. It is emotionally based. Man could thus determine and express his emotions.
- Taylor speaks from linguistically determined experiences of goods, and also the concrete experiences of 'faithfulness', "love", "pain", "helplessness", fulfilment".
- These ethical categories should be narratively articulated. This entails their relation to the life's experience in a broader sense of the word: they should be integrated and discussed in the individual and social context of daily life. So the good can be always discussed and proved

in the context of man's life: in the family, in the community, in the state and in the global society of the world.

- Bauman and Levinas represent the next step to the ethical anthropology respectively to the anthropological ethics.

Zygmund Bauman's postmodernity

I believe it was Zygmund Bauman (as Hannah Arendt) who dispelled all illusions about the modern systems and critically exposed the today's problems of man. He went through different experiences – he was a Marxist soldier, a communist leader, a professor and a political dissident. He was, like MacIntyre, a convinced Marxist and even more: he practiced the Marxian doctrine in the Soviet-Polish communist system. But he also experienced problems of the working class in a democratic system. Throughout his life he studied the major thinkers of our time. The most important is his experience with the communist totalitarian system, which has influenced his thinking and work to the present.

Bauman critically analysed modern systems and also some relativist (post)modern thinkers in regard to the free and autonomous man. He stressed that man should be liberated from the system's social pressure, and the postmodern thinking shows the ways to achieve this goal.

He is criticising modern systems which make man obedient and also inhuman. If systems try to urge man to oppress others, like the Nazis and communists did, he will do it. In his analysis of totalitarian thinking and the systems of communism and Nazism, especially in his work *Modernity and Ambivalence* (Bauman 1991), he stressed that all people are ready to do criminal acts and oppress others if they have been conditioned by pressure: "By the late twentieth century, all members of modern society had learned to live under a regime of constant surveillance, or at least to behave in a highly conformist manner as if they were indeed being monitored all the time." (Smith 1999, 139) Consequently, man should be liberated from obedience to the system and enabled for autonomous ethical acting. Modern societies have built the systems to control and to subdue man: "The elite imposes norms upon itself that are as strict as those obeyed by masses. Modern men and women conform to the rules governing the groups and organisations to which they belong. Work and effort are highly valued in themselves." (Smith 1991, 141) The Soviet and Nazi systems were not the only system to have perfected the total control over the life of people – several modern societies today are controlled by political oligarchy and mass media.

The modern order is "disorder". It is the order only for some people. The majority is excluded and can not participate in the sources of their daily life. The local authorities have lost their meaning. The poor and disadvantaged are given no choice, they are condemned to be poor and useless (Bauman 1998).

Thus ethics can only be the matter of an individual. It should be based on the primary experience of man that he needs other human beings. Yet, according to Hans Jonas, man should take the responsibility for the other. Bauman is like other postmodern thinkers convinced that only the person could be moral, ethics cannot be universalized. This comes as a shock, because the moral Self transgresses the system, because the moral responsibility for the Other is the basic extension of the moral Self. Bauman concludes that this fact does not confirm the relativity of the morality – unlike some postmodern thinkers and his critics who regarded this as inconsistency (Bauman 1995, 23-30). On the contrary – the reality of the moral Self is the basic reality of man. Man should be confirmed in this habitude and thus get his autonomy.

Bauman, together with Emanuel Levinas, advocates the full recognition of the Other. And "only those who died bringing help (for the Other, r. J.J) can say they have done enough." (Bauman 1993:80) The real prospect of ethics is to enable people to be autonomous and to take the responsibility for the Other.

Bauman in his *Postmodern Ethics* and other works constructs a more pessimistic view of the modern world which does not facilitate this ethical enterprise. The politicians have no real power to do it, nor are they ready to take the radical but necessary changes. They depend on the logic of economist (managers). We can thus only hope that the responsibility of the moral Self will be the base of ethical acting.

Bauman is critical of the reciprocity of ethical deeds. On this point he criticizes Rawls (justice as fairness) and Habermas ("the universalized responsibility of the taking possession as the universalized reciprocity" – "universalisierbare Reziprozität der Rollenübernahme als universalisierbare Reziprozität"), as well as the "reversibility of the perspectives" of Laurence Kohlberg (Bauman 1995, 328). He cites Vetlesen (1993, 25) who points out that only Levinas constructed really autonomous ethics. Through his ethics the rights of the unborn lives and the survival of humanity can be secured. He pointed out that the society of risk (Beck 1996) could overcome its problems only by adopting individual responsibility, as Hans Jonas (1979) stressed. As earlier said, Bauman is pessimistic about the success of this undertaking in the present political and societal conditions of our world.

Conclusion

The main problem of the ethics in modernity and postmodernity is the search for Self and its ability to perform its moral task. This means establishing Self as the source of man's ethical ability. Only from himself can man act ethically, but he has to foresee (Prometheus) his conditions of life. This project is rather a practical one, not merely theoretical. Ethics thus cannot be a scientific or systematic – a modern enterprise, but only the ethics of an autonomous person, the ethics of an individual in his responsibility to the Other - a postmodern enterprise. Bauman, Levinas, and Vetlesen point out that only irreciprocal responsibility can be the guarantee that everybody can live and survive. The reality is that man comes to this world and can survive in this world only through the Other. This announcement can make possible the life of the Other and secure the future of human race.

3. DIALOGUE – NECESSITY FOR A PERSON

Societal Conditions

In the post-communist countries dialogue within the society proves to be a problem. The antagonisms of the former totalitarian system are still present and the Manichaean tendencies prevail, pushing people in permanent conflicts. The significant example is the Slovenian society. We have reached good organisational and economic conditions, yet the antagonistic tendencies in the society have not ceased. The willingness for dialogue is lacking. It takes much energy to reach solutions acceptable for all, to cooperate and to establish common national interests. The sediments of "class enemies" from the communist regime are still present in the mentality of people, preventing cooperation and normal human relations in media, in politics and daily life, while antagonisms make societal dialogue more difficult.

Both the post-communist countries and in the countries with a long democratic tradition are developing the postmodern individualistic mentality. The man increasingly develops a sense of individuality and has no sense of societal relations. The man isolates himself in his own personal world and is not willing to communicate and share his own world with others. The economic and productive haste takes more and more of his time, so he has no time for human relations. The psychological emphasis of individuality also cultivates the egoistic mentality. It is stimulated by the economic liberalism, which has established the mentality of competition, exclusion and isolation. The man is less and less prepared to cooperate and share his life.

Again, this mentality is especially powerful in the post-communist countries. In the communist period the people in these countries had to share their lives and goods and they did not have the possibility to organize their own lives. After the fall of communism, people used the opportunity to form and organize their own life and to get rid of the constant pressure the totalitarian regime had exerted on their personal lives.

On the other hand, the world is increasingly becoming a unity, particularly through economic and productive processes. Media has turned the world a global village. The means of communication connect people and make it possible to contact everybody anytime and to share all everyday things. Everybody is kept informed about what is happening in the world, but this information is filtered and selected by those who manage media, so this selection is discriminatory. As Ottmar Fuchs points out, many events are thus eliminated. Some people are discriminated and eliminated from the picture. Fuchs stresses the opposition between the politically motivated and the real problems of the man (Fuchs 2007). The terrorist attack on the World Trade Centre in New York was politically opportune and attracted much public interest. The death of millions women, men and children in Africa or in other parts of the third world does not earn such publicity.

The communication in the modern liberally oriented world is a problem because it is an individualistic one. The man is eager to solve his own problems, yet he is not prepared to share his own life and participate in the community. This is the one of the greatest problems of the so-called postmodern society. The world is at the same time still pushed into various conflicts which threaten to destroy the social order and mankind as such.

Despite globalisation, the readiness for dialogue in the world is growing slowly. Manichaean tendencies prevail, pushing people in permanent conflicts. The willingness for dialogue is lacking. The development of the postmodern individualistic mentality is twofold. Man not only increasingly develops a sense of individuality and his rights, but also loses a sense of societal relations. Man isolates himself in his own personal world and is not willing to communicate and share his own world with others. The economic and productive haste takes more and more of his time, so he has no time for human relations. The psychological emphasis of individuality also cultivates egoistic mentality. It is stimulated by the economic liberalism, which has established the mentality of competition, exclusion and isolation. The man is less and less prepared to cooperate and share his life. The unregulated envy caused by the economic competition increases societal tensions, so lives of individuals and groups are more and more out of control. There is an emptiness, which could be easily misused for manipulations by media and politics.

On the other hand, the world is increasingly becoming a unity, also through economic and productive processes. Media has turned the world into a global village. The means of communication connect people and make it possible to contact everybody anytime and to share all everyday things. Everybody is kept informed about what is happening in the world, but this information is filtered and selected by managers of economy, politics and media, so this selection is discriminatory. As Ottmar Fuchs points out, many events are thus eliminated. Some people are discriminated and eliminated from the picture. Fuchs stresses the opposition between the politically motivated and the real problems of man (Fuchs 2007). The terrorist attack on the World Trade Centre in New York was politically opportune and attracted much public interest. The deaths of millions of women, men and children in Africa or in other parts of the third world do not earn such publicity.

The communication in the modern liberally oriented world is a problem because it is individualistic one. Man is eager to solve his own problems, yet he is not prepared to share his own life and participate in the community. The problems of the globalised society are very complicated and the world is pushed into different conflicts which threaten to destroy the social order and mankind as such. Men with economic and political power have more opportunities than ordinary men and social differentiation is increasing.

Clashes of the civilisations

It is understandable, as Samuel Huntington (1993) pointed out, that this globalised world tends to produce antagonisms. In the age of media all differences and antagonisms of the modern world are becoming increasingly obvious. In this way the tensions in the world become more and more public and this brings the risk of clashes between different groups; between national, religious and ideological communities.

Man's perennial problem is that he gravitates toward antagonisms. He tends to develop the mentality of Manichaeism, which in turn produces the mentality of exclusion. There are two worlds: the world of Light, of Goodness, and the world of Darkness, of Evil. People are divided as the good and the bad. Media further intensify these opposites of the modern world (Schulze 2003, 67). These opposites in the world should sustain the balance and tension which make it possible to maintain the world's political order. It is the problematic points that sustain these balances, and innocent people have to take the consequences of the world strife, as in the case of Darfur and other places. According to René Girard, the society is looking for a scapegoat (Girard 1987). The scapegoat should be weak, so the society could survive, because he cannot resist against the will of the majority, which decides about the lives of all.

The Darwinian Paradigm

Joachim Bauer (2006) criticises in his book *Prinzip Menschlichkeit* ("A Principle of Humanity") Darwin's "war of nature" as a principle of un-humanity. According to Bauer, man's genes are more willing to cooperate than to fight. The man is inherently disposed to cooperate and not to exclude others. There are no proofs that man's genes are by nature made to exclude others. On the contrary: Bauer as a physician confirms that genes are willing to cooperate. Aggression is caused by lack of cooperation or love.

He rejects the concept that man and the whole nature are inherently determined to struggle for life, and that this struggle means the war of all against all. Yet this is exactly how Richard Dawkins (2006) revives Darwinism – by stressing that the "selfish gene" directs our actions. The man has "a selfish device", which means the subject is considered as a "selfish device" (Dawkins 2006, Ch. 5). The most important discovery in connection with this is according to Dawkins the Theory of Evolution by Charles Darwin, who thorough this theory enabled a new view of human history. The man should be engaged in the same struggle. There are fights between generations (Ch. 8), the sexes (Ch. 9), there are family disputes, there are struggles between races, nations etc.

Yet according to Bauer, Darwin and Dawkins found out just a part of the whole story of the life in nature (Bauer 2006, 95). Darwin's theory was strongly influenced by Thomas Robert Malthus (1766-1834). Darwin was also racially prejudiced; he favoured the so-called cultured nations. According to Bauer, the theory contains many simplifications in regard to nature. However, Darwin had strongly influenced psychologists and other natural scientists at the end of the 19th century. His racism was accepted by many German psychologists and influenced the idea of a pure race and the tendencies to expel the weak from the society (Bauer 2006, 110). Dawkins operates on the basis of Darwin's premises, while Bauer regards the model of Dawkins as science-fiction made to appear as science (Bauer 2006, 135ff.).

A very influential perpetuator of Darwin's theory was Marxism. According to Engels, Darwin's theory finds its fulfilment in the natural dialectic process. This process is manifested in the fight of the opposites. A revolution, as a driving force of this process, functions by excluding others. There should be only one party, only one class and only one type of man. It led to the big revolutions of the last centuries, which destroyed innumerable lives and thoroughly degraded people. The entire generations have been suffering because of this man's experiment. The story of Marxism ended in 1990, confirming its own unnaturalness.

The next perpetuator of the modern struggle to survive is the liberalistic economic and social system. Economism, as a deviant form of the economic and social doctrine, influenced the rivalry in the postmodern society. The strongest have the possibility to survive, the weak have to perish. There are many variations of this system in the modern society. All this influenced struggle in society which culminated in the societal perturbations of the 20th century. Today they have more sophisticated forms of political and economic exclusion and discrimination. Wars, revolutions and power struggles marked and still mark this period of history, and many consequences of this so-called imperialistic era are still felt.

This is the reason why religious institutions fought and still fight the systems of modernity – liberalistic states, organisations and other powerful institutions. Churches are in general against the modern acquisitions. The same reason guides some Christian and Islamic religious leaders to oppose modern political institutions. At the same time they use the benefits of the modern world. So it is understandable that clashes among different groups appear, especially among different ideological or religious systems and political systems. These are the reasons for the tension between religious and political systems and the present politisation of religions. Religion becomes more and more a political factor. This is today a particular problem, as the economy dominates entire political, social and cultural life of man. The economy reduces man to economic interests. Political orders and even religious doctrines are subordinated to these interests, so religion will become not only a political but also an economic factor. Maybe the difficulties in economic developments will change it, but this is now a fact that influences our daily life.

It is quite clear that the social system could not work well if we are not prepared to cooperate, to combine old traditions with new demands, spiritual needs with the needs of our bodies, connect the old generation with the new, link the system of consumption with the idea of social justice, the life of the present generation with the lives of those yet unborn, one nation with another and one system another. Religions have an anthropological basis for giving people the reason to cooperate and work together. Man is an ethical being and cannot function without tradition, without connections with others, his ancestors and his progeny. This means that cooperation, dialogue and regard for others represent a sine qua non for humankind.

Toward a dialogue

Bauer stresses: "The model of Darwin neglects the basic role of cooperation, which is the beginning of all biology."(Bauer 2006, 128) He found out that not only in genes but also in other areas of life the cooperation is the basis of life. Without the cooperation, the basic biological functions could not be sustained. This is not only Bauer's conclusion, it is acknowledged also by different biologists, psychologists, sociologists and other experts. An important example is children who grew up with animals. The consequence of this was that they couldn't live in normal human relations. Similarly, the children who grew up in abnormal conditions couldn't develop normal feelings; they aggressively related to other people and had in adulthood difficulties with relating to other people. They needed psychological care to help them cooperate.

According to Bauer, the life tends toward cooperation. The whole genealogy of life is based on genes. Organisms are much more complex. The genes are "under acute control of the whole organism." (Bauer 2006, 158) Genes thus work in cooperation with other functions of an organism - especially important and influential among them is human consciousness. So genes are willing to cooperate with the internal and external facts of life. In case of man, nothing can be accomplished without cooperation. The biological and psychological components are formed by environment. The genes are thus not only the basic codes of development, they are also caused by the "biochemical depositness" (Bauer 2006, 163). This means cooperation is the basis of biogenesis and without cooperation human life is not possible, since people are beings of dialogue. Human genes are influenced by environment and there are many variations of this cooperation. The cooperation is an important factor of evolution. Economists are today emphasising the importance of cooperation. Reinhard Selten is the author of the so-called *"Urexperiment der Spieltheorie"* ("The prior experiment of the theory of game") (Bauer 2006, 178). Cooperation is so important for man that, as Bauer stresses, our brains do not agree with uncooperative unfairness; they consider such behaviour punishable (Bauer 2006, 185).

Bauer goes on to show that dialogue is an important basis of the living nature and especially of man, because man depends on his environment more that other living beings - he depends on his own species. According to different researches, between 70 and 90 % of man's activities are directed by dialogue.

The observation of our daily lives seems not to confirm this truth. Bauer lists several examples from childhood and from different occupations, even from economy. All this confirms that the man is a being of dialogue, despite the examples from our daily lives seem to negate this fundamental truth.

A being of dialogue

The man is a being who seeks attention. As the MacIntyre (1999) says, the man is a dependent rational animal (Žalec 2005, 117). The man depends on others; he wants to see and wants to be seen (Bauer 2006, 191). The respect he gains and the respect he gives depend on the relation between human beings, and this is the question of emotional sympathy. To understand this, he must prove his motives and intentions and the motives and intentions of others, because they differ from each other, so these differences should be taken into account. It is helpful to undergo the process of dialogue. Bauer stresses the importance of dialogue for personal, social, political, economical life and the life of the man as such (Bauer 2006, 200). The differences between people on one hand make dialogue possible, while on the other hand they make it much more difficult, differences have to be overcome through dialogue in order to solve the problems of daily life. Dialogue is the only way to solve the man's problems.

The man is a symbolic being, a being of language. He could solve his life's problems through dialogue with partners. The child could come into (or could reach) the man's life only through others (Juhant 2006, 19ff.). This means that he/she can learn the language and can through dialogue with others come to feel and to express his/her emotions. To become a wo/man, it is necessary to learn the language and learn to feel as a wo/man. The children growing up among animals could not develop human abilities, because they could not feel as humans. This dependence of the man continues throughout one's life. We are always "dependent rational animals" (MacIntyre 1999), we need each other not only to perform our daily tasks but even more to accomplish our emotional life. As deMause points out, the emotional life is not a matter of a single person but of a nation, too (de Mause 2005, chap. 5). A person takes part in the fantasies of the entire nation. The prejudices among different nations are thus an obstacle to reach understanding and dialogue between them. The Balkans is a grave example of the persistent problems that are anchored in the collective consciousness of these nations. But there are other examples in Europe and elsewhere: Spain, Great Britain, Russia etc. If people have to live under pressure for a long time, this unfailingly leave scars. "The behaviour of the man in the society can be shortsighted and uninformed, but never unreasonable, self-destructive and cruel – it is not human." (deMause 2005, 70)

This can be overcome and solved only through dialogue. Person is a being of dialogue because he/she belongs to other person, as the Bible says: "It is not good that the man should be alone; I will make him helper fit for him." (Gen 2, 18) The person cannot be alone because he/she needs other person. The child cannot grow up without other persons. The language is not only a means to organise daily life but much more – a means to share emotional states and to acknowledge mutual dependence and possibilities to cooperate. Bauer and other biologists and psychologist stress that the real cause of aggression and other deviations is the lack of cooperation and dialogue. So the main problem of an individual and the social history of man is the lack of understanding. Serious destructive psychogenic reactions arise if a person's and nations' basic needs in regard to emotions and their expression are not met. To avoid or to overcome his/her psychic shortcomings, a person has to engage in dialogue and share his/her emotive life.

Dialogue in the family

As the family is the man's native place of man, it is also the native place of dialogue. The family provides a person with the first symbolic forms which enable him/her to recognise the world around him/her. The first years of the child's life are very important because during this period the entire psychological and syntactic structures are formed. The person is during this period enabled to establish "normal" human relations. If the development is in this period due to some reasons inhibited, this causes troubles throughout one's life. So the family is the decisive factor in everybody's life. Education is discussed widely and incessantly, yet these discussions tend to forget the importance of establishing good relationships with children in which they can appropriately develop their emotional life. "Die Intentitätsbildung geschieht in einem internen, psychologischen und einem externen, sozialen Prozess. Die verantwortete Auseinandersetzung mit dem Schicksal, mit anderen Menschen, mit uns selbst, hält diesen Prozess in Gang." (Kast 2003, 23) The identity of a person is the ability to harmonize his/her external claims with his/her internal attitudes. The child acquires these attitudes through other persons, parents and society. They are internalised by a person in the form of values and enable him/her to master his/her life and to homologise the tensions between the austerity and his/her inner life.

To perform this task, a person needs permanent exchange with other persons to prove his own attitudes. One's identity always depends on other persons. As Kast points out, if somebody wants to be a genius, he needs some people to certificate him as a genius (Kast 2003, 99). The family is a primary place to acquire this ability in which a person learns to manage his/her problems and to maintain the balance of his/her life. It is essential that a person can tell his/her own story, to express himself/herself, her/his own feelings, as postmodern thinkers emphasise. To tell his/her story means to carry out a discourse about his/her problems. To discuss means to regulate in a human way differences and tensions between his/her emotional life and the lives of others. If this is carried out successfully within the family, a person has the best basis and preparation to carry out dialogue within society. Because the family is conditioned by the societal circumstances, the ability for dialogue has a social, cultural, religious and civilisational background.

The present society is unfavourable for personal relations, thus creating unfavourable conditions for communication, and this causes serious disturbances within the family. Children could be enabled for the intensive emotional exchange, yet they are often pushed in the virtual world of media and internet. This has lasting consequences for their emotional life. They are not well prepared for human communication.

These are serious obstacles for dialogue among young people today. The socio-economic conditions also stimulate impersonal relationships.

Society, culture and religions

The world of today depends very much on economic conditions. It means that economic conditions of life are directing our daily life. The economic process determines human relations. This often manifests as the so-called economic globalism. It means economic processes are prevailing and life is reduced to them. All human relations are determined by them. The system of advertising supports this and people have to organise their lives in the manner it dictates. This brings severe problems:

1. The way of life is determined by economic and not by human relations. It is not important how the man lives but how he consumes. The industry, for example the pharmaceutical industry, makes products whose sole purpose is to be consumed. The whole system of life is dictated by the process of production, the real human needs are thus subjugated to it.

2. The second problem is that the economic logic tends to produce more and more. So the main role in these processes is taken over by managers. They have to decide what sort of production will be carried out and where, in order to get the best output and make more money. People and their needs (also economic needs) are not relevant, their role is reduced to supporting the best system of production.

3. The whole life is productive, competitive, and people are ousting each other. Those capable have better chances, while less capable and disabled people cannot keep up with the competition. As John Rawls (1999, 53) points out, they should be supported, but the system of production does not allow it. Poverty is spreading in the today's world, the gap between the rich and the poor is ever wider. Dialogue is under such circumstances more important than ever, yet it is increasingly difficult to carry it out. The protests of the so-called antiglobalists express these problems, but the meeting in Heiligendamm confirms that the dialogue on big differences in the modern society is a major problem. We can list many other problems, such as Darfur, Palestine, Chechnya, the Basque country, etc.

4. The economic system of production and competition causes pollution and brings problems for future generations.

This all aggravates national, political and international problems of our world, which could be solved only through patient, persistent and open dialogue. This dialogue is possible only if we are prepared to cooperate and not to exclude anybody from these relations. It must be carried out in a human way, not on the economic basis. Humanity will be realised on ethical grounds (Juhant 2003, 6). If we are willing to meet each other in a human way, we can get the most human results. We have no other way. It is just the question whether we will take the opportunity for dialogue first or only after conflicts among us have already escalated. All wars, all strife and all lack of understanding among men could in the end be solved by dialogue.

The religion - an anthropological factor

The religion is thus an important anthropological factor in man's life. The enlightenment encouraged the studies of religions at the same time it opened the one-sided (reductionist) status of religions, which has survived to this day. Various reductionisms – sociological, psychological, scientific, political – limited the religion from their individual perspectives. However, theories of religion gradually adopted the anthropological approach, because man is a religious being and the religion covers a very influential dimension of man, his transcendent openness. But there are still relicts of the enlightenment in our cultural, scientific and political world. The religion is seen as a vehiculum (Kant), as an appendage, which should be indispensable for ordinary people and their safety, while nobility can do without. Close to this is the definition of religion by Durkheim, who pointed out that religion is an integer system of beliefs and practices, "which the people combine in one community, namely Church." (Lavrič/Flere 2008) Religion is necessary to uphold the social order. So different enlightened circles aren't ready to accept this view of religion and acknowledge that religion is an important part of life for all people. It is a question of the wholeness (completeness) of man's personality.

Religion as an important part (view) of man causes many misunderstandings among scientists, politicians and opinion makers. Maybe religion is going to be a growing political factor, but the social and personal consciousness still maintains that religious ideas are not compatible with the modern "way of life". Today this combines with the problem of man's means of living. Already the Dutch theorist of religion Gerardus van der Leeuw (1890-1950) pointed out the phenomenological or the anthropological view of religion. He stresses the religious experience of man, which declares man as a being in a relationship with the other. Man knows himself as a being who is given to the other. There is an "eccentric structure of man" (W. Panneberg), which means "to be at other". Religion is a belief that all activities of man are solved within a safety framework (H. Plessner; Schmitz 1984, 156-166). It is an experience that a person is given by the other and at least by the Other (with capital letter, Juhant 2000).

Today there are many theorists stressing this dimension of religion. There are many different forms of experiencing religion, like the one of William James (2002), on one hand, and of different fundamentalism, authoritarianism etc., on the other. There is more openness for the phenomena of religion among sociologists, but there is more criticism of the so-called statutory religions. The reasons are the postmodern fear of institutions and the very influential connection between religion, especially Islam, and political power. In these circumstances there is a good orientation toward an objective estimation of religion by the internationally renowned Slovenian sociologist Thomas Luckmann. He says religion is manifested as an "invisible religion". In the same sense I understand the so-called Weltethos ("world ethos") by Hans Küng. There are not many possibilities to make a visible platform as a fundament of different religions, yet there is an important common anthropological ground. According to Gandhi all religious people can come together if they are ready to deepen their religious forms. "Religion has a history, and what counts as a religion, and what does not in any given context depends on different configurations of power and authority." (Cavanaugh 2009, 9)

The religion is an invisible ground of man – this was pointed out by modern philosophers of language, like Richard M. Hare (1919-...). This ground enables us to live safely and to live our lives as human beings. As beings of language, we can express these "invisible thoughts" through our language.

And to apply a language means to dialogize, to take part in lives of others. The experience of the other could be obtained by man only through dialogue. The anthropological analysis of religion shows that it is a constitutive ground of openness and readiness of man to express himself as a being of dialogue. Jews and Christian knows the famous sentences in the Old Testament by Jeremiah 17, 5 and 7: "Cursed is the man who trusts in man and makes flesh his arm ...Blessed is the man who trusts in the Lord, whose trust is the Lord..." It doesn't mean that the man shouldn't trust anybody. In contrary: we should be empathic to others, but the human trust is a limited one, because the man is a vulnerable being. Every dialogue of man is limited by man as a terminal being. The Lord is in fact the one who can deliver the man from his entanglement in himself or his earthly dimensions. Faith is the ground of the true relationships among people. Faith helps and enables man to take all things on this world as penultimate. The problem of the Enlightenment critique of religion is that it limits the knowledge and all activities of an individual, who can't fulfil these ambitions. The truth couldn't be found on the surface. To find it, we should be ready to acknowledge the other and to kneel down before God. The truth is beyond daily procedures, man has to open his spiritual eyes to reach it: H. J-. Kouschel quotes words of the well-known philosopher of the Frankfurt school Max Horkheimer: "Theology means the consciousness that the world is an appearance, it is not the absolute truth, is not the ultimate. Theology is – one has to be careful with words here - the hope that despite all injustices in this world, it will not stay like this, that injustice is not final, it is the expression of languishing for this, that the murder couldn't triumph over the innocent victim." (Kuschel 2008, 52)

Theology is an expression of the limitedness of this world and at the same time a criticism about the unjust conditions in this world. Because of this, it is difficult to find the truth of ourselves, of others and of the real circumstances of this world. Dialogue is thus necessarily coming our way. But worldly powers are very strong and strongly hinder this process in order to maintain status quo. Even more – we all hinder this process to persist in this state. Today there are many obstacles which prevent changing unjust conditions in personal and social life, in politics, economy and in everyday life. Politicians and economists produce public opinion, which in media conceals the real problems of man, and adapt the streams of events to their political, economic and sometimes quite personal interests, even their caprices. Even religion can be abused for these purposes. This has been a problem throughout history, yet the present circumstances in the world are much more complicated.

Consequently, dialogue is more difficult, yet obviously needed more than ever. It is today a sine qua non of man's survival.

Religious dialogue and critics of religion

If the things are the way I have described them, it is necessary for man to accept the way of dialogue in religious relations. Like other kinds of dialogue, the religious dialogue is a difficult task, because man is a limited being, often covered with hard and firmly ossified structures. Pope John Paul II called this "the structures of evil." (John Paul II. 1987) Personal and societal life of the people are structured, but if the structures don't serve man, they cause negative effects. There are many such structures of man's life today and we have to ask ourselves whether our economical and political development in its different modern dimensions serves the majority of people of this world. If the majority of people are not invited to participate in the benefits of this life, this development should be questioned and criticised. Already Plato knew that the powerful don't use justice. It is difficult to attract rulers to dialogue, but maybe all people, including the leaders of this world, have to take into account that this world is in danger (and they, as well), if we are not ready to examine its problems together. Through dialogue we have to find solutions for all people, because our common future is at stake. This can happen, if everybody becomes aware of his own limitedness. Only if we are all prepared to accept this, our limitedness, will we understand that man is "a dependent rational animal", as MacIntyre says. Today we are living more superficially, sometimes we are caught in the structures of our modern life and we are not willing to question them. But this is also an important question concerning our religious relations, because religious structures are in the same danger of becoming inhuman and supporting the structures of evil, if religions aren't ready to open the grounds of man's existence and merely keep up appearances. As human beings we need openness towards one another and only thus can we deepen our views, including religious views. We need to accept each other as partners in this project and to see it as a very important religious project.

The obstacles of religious dialogue

A very important problem, which results from the anthropological view of religion, is the problem of violence. Jean-Pierre Depuy quoting René

Girard stresses that the ambivalence of rivalry has its roots in nearness. A rival is at the same time an example for himself and his opponent, because none of the two can obtain cqual level of recognition. The traditional monotheistic religions: Judaism, Christianity and Islam have been rivals throughout history. Problems of rivalry are common in the history of our religions. It is very difficult to elaborate on the complexity of these problems, but they display, as Hans Küng explains, certain common denominators.

In regard to Christianity – Hans Küng compares the catholic tradition to other religions: "The traditional Catholic position up to the twentieth century – prepared for in the early Christian centuries by Origen, Cyprian and Augustine - is generally known: *extra ecclesiam nulla salus,* no salvation outside the Church. *Extra ecclesiam nullus propheta,* no prophet outside the church. The ecumenical council of Florence in 1442 issued an unequivocal definition. 'The Holy Roman Church... firmly believes, confesses and proclaims that no one outside the Catholic Church, whether pagan or Jew or unbeliever or one separated from the church, will participate in eternal life; rather he will fall into the eternal fire prepared for the devil and his angels, unless he joins it (the Catholic Church) before his death!'" And he concludes: "For Catholics, doesn't that settle the claim of Islam? Fore more than 1200 years it seemed to." (Küng 2007, 55)

Küng stresses three characteristics of Islam: "exclusivity, theocracy and militancy":

"*Exclusivity*: On the basis of the treaty of Medina, non-Muslims too were originally members of Mohammed's community, especially Jews, so strongly represented in Medina. However, after the successive elimination of the Jewish tribes the community became exclusively Muslim. At first, Jews and Christian were tolerated in Arabia, until they were driven out under the second caliph Umar. He wanted Arabia to be purely Muslim. This is decisive point for understanding Islam: so initially the intensity of the religious and political following of the prophet differed considerably – and the Qur'an tells us there were also some 'hypocrites' (unreliable people), as well as the true 'believers' – soon it was no longer disputed that the whole of the religious and the political life of the state was subject to laws which did not come from man but from God." (Küng 2007, 159)

"*Theocracy:* here the difference from Christianity is evident. The Christian community or church was outside the state (whether Jewish or Roman), even in conflict with it, and sometimes persecuted by it. Even in Byzantine mode of a 'symphony' of throne and altar it remained completely distinct from the state... Things were quite different right from the beginning in the Muslim community, a 'divine state', where there is no separation between state and religion." (Küng 2007, 159) Despite this theoretical observation, we can see that faith in some orthodox, protestant and even catholic forms in practice took the indicia of the "divine state", it means the sociological effects were often the same, if we critically observe these examples of our Christian history.

"*Militancy*: here a further difference from the Christian community or church is striking. The Christian community is committed, by the message, behaviour and fate of its founder, to non violence – despite what violent "Christian" rulers (emperors, kings, bishops and popes) and believers did with the original Christian ideal once Christianity became a state religion. The Islamic community, in which state and religion coincide from the beginning, is quite different: Mohammed understood it as a fighting community which was allowed to fight with swords. Indeed, war as a means of politics was not only affirmed in principle, but, when necessary, waged without any great inhibitions. Thus from its origins Islam has had a militant character, fighting for God – in this respect it is closer to early Judaism and its 'Yahweh wars' than to early Christianity." (Küng 2007, 160)

But there are enough grounds for the other side of our religions:

1. The early Jewish constitution as a "religious democracy": Israel, the prophetic pioneer and its message amidst the surrounding dynasties.
2. The Christian profession of a pluralistic "church in places" with its constant strife for diversity in unity and against sectarian schisms and tendencies of a "divine centralism".
3. The Islamic Ummah amidst the united nations of the modern world. The various traditions of Islam in a common plead for human rights and religious freedom in modern states.
4. Buddhist attempts to promote interior life as an universal means of communication. The silent resistance against violence, usurpation and exploitation (deceit).

The film by the Dutch politician Geert Widlers *Fitna* became an answer in the film of a blogger from Saudi Arabia *Shisma*. We all have to confess there was much violence in own religious traditions. As human beings we all need the acknowledgement and mercy of God and of the people of God. The life of people in this world is more and more complicated. As religious men we have a duty to contribute to solving these problems. These are our challenges. It is our duty to show and to confess the anthropological, the human contents of our religions and to confirm God's love for all people.

I'm convinced that the basic aims of all religions are peace, reconciliation and salvation of all people. This could be reached only through open dialogue among members of religions and through their dialogue with God. We need religious communities with true faith. Communities which are free from external pressures and which through internal exchange enrich and promote their religious heritage. The Slovenian word for riches derives from the word God. The wealth of communities comes from the wealth of their experience of God's and man's love. It could be reached by the exchange of opinions, prayers and decisions within a community, in dialogue with others and with God.

Because cultural development in the modern world is in many ways problematic for people and their religious faith global cultural and political development in the world causes problems in religious communities. On the other hand we all benefit from this modern world, which is the consequence of liberal people, democracy, technical developments and profits. It is a very challenging time. As religious people, we have to oppose "Mächten und Gewalten" (powers and forces) of this world. The answer to the uncertain situation is dialogue, based on recognition and respect of the cultural, ethic, racial, gender and religious differences of people with whom we are in contact (Svetelj, 130). Such dialogue reinforces our readiness to cooperate and facilitate benefits for all people. We need to overcome our earthly entanglements with ourselves and with things, and live our faith sincerely. It is not only the task of ordinary men, but also the task of scientists, politicians, media people, economists, of all people of good will, and especially of believers in God. People can't trust only one another, they have to trust God if they want to solve the pressing problems people face. It is necessary to overcome manipulative ways of thinking and acting (even religious) and be ready and open for dialogue. The crucial problem in this dialogue is economic exploitation. Muslems are not the only second-class citizens of this world; more and more other people are becoming second-class citizens. Among these are many believers who are oppressed by other believers. We should oppose this and try to free all "the untouchables". Gandhi said they are particularly loved by God, and we, believers, have to testify to this divine love for all people of this world: especially for people who are the target of discrimination, the lost and the weak, thus showing the anthropological value of our religions.

Bosnia and Herzegovina and the Balkans

"Kosovo is a wonder, as it is a wonder regarding all that happened in the Balkans through the centuries." (Gaiser 2007, 55) The long lasting and permanent problems of history condense in the Balkans. There were many unsolved disparities between the Christian East and West, between the Slavic, Roman and Germanic cultures and between the Christian and the Islamic religions and cultures. Here dialogue here faces a difficult task.

It began in the Middle Ages with the Bogomils. They came from Bulgaria and Macedonia to Bosnia, which became their home. Later the Cathars fled from France where they were persecuted by the Crusaders (Pope Innocent III, +1217). Under the Turkish dominion they slowly accepted Islam. Bosnia, where the First World War started, was the crossroads between domain of the Soviet (communist) and the Western democratic world (Yalta). Bosnia and Herzegovina was a test of the fall of communism. Bosnia and Herzegovina and the Balkans today represent, in special way, a test of the possibilities for dialogue between the Islamic and the Christian world.

Whether this troublesome point of the European politics will be solved by dialogue, and thus by human devices, or it will lead to a new brutal conflict depends on the willingness of politicians to cooperate. As can be seen in the case of Kosovo, East and West perceive the situation quite differently. We can see that the differences between both sides of Europe are still present. Some of these differences concern the status and level of democracy, national, social, religious and cultural mentality, the art of dialogue. But the wars could not solve any problems, as we have seen. Will dialogue now prevail, will the problems be solved in a human manner? The policy of peace requires openness and readiness to listen to each other and to understand the said differences. The art of dialogue is to understand and realise them. It seems that the policies concerning Balkan, Kosovo and Bosnia and Herzegovina depend too much on the interests of the USA and Russia, so the people of Kosovo, Serbia and Bosnia and Herzegovina was again victims of these policies. We can nevertheless take part in this process by arguing for dialogue everywhere. If we are people of dialogue, politicians cannot work against us this way, as they depend on our votes.

Christian responsibility for dialogue

J. H. H. Weiler stresses the meaning and role of the Christians in the process of dialogue in Europe: "The spiritual challenges are great. But this chapter and even this discussion should end with a message of hope. As we have said, the *preamble* to the European constitution ends with the confirmation of the conviction that the European Union is 'a special area of human hope'. That will come true if we learn how to cross the long bridge of modernity and postmodernity without endangering human dignity and love. It is important that we do not feel fear in the process." (Weiler 2005, 151)

In my book *Globalisirung, Kirche und postmoderner Mensch* I stressed that dialogue should distinguish members the Catholic Church (Juhant 2005, 167). Dialogue should be carried out in the community of saints (*eccelsia*). The Holy Trinity is the measure of the Christian relations, and as God is dialogue, the church should be a special place of dialogue. The community of the Church and its organisation do not carry out this task zealously enough, yet it is an essential point of its survival.

Stanko Gerjolj (2006), in his book *Live, Work, Love,* points out the pedagogical value of the examples from the Old Testaments for solving interpersonal problems and establishing dialogue.

If dialogue, as a basic human device for solving human problems, prevails in the Church and in the society, then there is hope for humane policies and humane world in Kosovo, in Bosnia and Herzegovina, Darfur, Palestine etc.

4. ETHICAL DIALOGUE, LINK BETWEEN PHILOSOPHY, SCIENCE, AND RELIGION

Introduction

All man's actions are regulated by man's symbolic capacity. This opens man's transcendental ability and with it his transcendental basis, which can be realised only in dialogue, even scientific work is a product of this dialogue. "…scientific pluralism emerges as normal and natural, and ought to allow for conversations between people from different traditions or cultural domains." (Van Huyssteen 2006, 33) The same holds true for different sciences, philosophies and theologies. So philosophy, theology and different sciences should be open to dialogue and be partners in this dialogue. Man as an ethical being is by his nature a partner in such dialogue. Since scientists in biotechnical research are not willing "to ask" an embryo about his/her participation in the process – even an embryo is a subject in this process – they are ignoring this fundamental ethical rule. The researches are in this case also not willing to preserve the dialogue between different sciences, philosophies and theologies. The researchers of this kind are thus usually limited to the experimental-technical, economical or other aspects, and the researchers are neither willing to participate in this fundamental personal and ethical dialogue, nor to preserve human rights. Behind all man's actions are limited views of the world (Gelhaus 2006). These horizons can be widened only by ethical qualification, which should, according to Kant, respect the ethical postulates: the soul, the world and God (Kant 1956, B870). Today it is important to stress not only the deontological but also the dialogical aspect of these postulates.

The relation between faith and science became topical in discussions between Christian and pagan philosophers in the early Middle Ages. It reached its peak with the Aristotelian commentaries in the High Middle Ages, when the topic was developed to the perfection that remained unmatched for quite some time. This question was reiterated with the development of science in the New Ages, particularly with the promotion of Thomism in the papal encyclical of Pope Leo XIII *Aeterni Patris*, which was issued on the 4th of August 1879. The aim of Thomists was in fact to restore the metaphysical order of the Middle Ages. The Catholic philosophers tried to make the universal and unique conceptual Christian world. The renewal of the Catholic philosophy appeared at the end of the 19th century and in the first part of the 20th century (Coreth et al. 1988). On the other hand, the science of that time was influenced by thc (German) Kulturkampf (clash of cultures) after 1870. The period after the Enlightenment was under strong influence of the so-called "Enlightenment science", which means the science without any presuppositions (Gadamer 1993, 434). The consequences of this prejudice have remained in the discussions about the power of science to this day. This served as a basis for Christian theologians and philosophers – but also for other, more anthropological oriented thinkers when they again tried to regulate and to unite the two worlds: the world of science and the world of faith.

The Arabs in the Middle Ages brought Aristotle to the Western world and thus discussion began among Christian scholars about the Aristotelian scientific view of the world. Because the scientific view was increasingly important, scholars tried to confer the faith the status of science: *in statu scientiae*. They decided that faith too should be regarded in a scientific manner. So they made the Christian faith competitive with the science. "Mit seiner wissenschaftstheoretischen Konzeption entspricht Thomas von Aquin den berechtigten Ansprüchen der Vertreter der Fakultät der freien Künste, die die Selbständigkeit von Wissenschaft und Philosophie beanspruchen, und er entspricht auch der historischen Situation einer Gesellschaft, die sich den anderen Kulturen öffnet und eine gemeinsame vernünftige Basis für das Gespräch mit diesen sucht, während andere meinten, diese Begegnung kriegerisch durchführen zu müssen. Er entspricht aber auch den Forderungen seiner Kirche und seiner Ordensgemeinschaft, die an einer Gruppe von Wahrheiten festhalten will, die außerhalb des Bereiches der Philosophie liegen." (Schupp 2003, 387) This openness of the Christian faith and its scientific accommodation enabled theology to be competitive with other scientific languages, as Schupp points out: "Was Thomas hier unternimmt ist das folgende: Er versucht, verschiedene Ausdrücke eines *physikalischen* bzw. Naturphiloso-phischen oder metaphysischen *Weltbildes* mit der dazugehörigen Sprache einem Ausdruck aus der *religiösen Sprache* zuzuordnen. Dass es sich um ein Problem der Sprache handelt, ist ihm ganz klar: es geht um etwas, dass die Menschen ‚Gott' nennen." (Schupp 2003, 398)

At the time of Aquinas the problem of different languages existed; he was trying to combine them: the scientific (of nature), the metaphysical and the religious language. Thomas and some other scholastic theologians wanted to combine these languages, because this suited their unified picture of the world. They tried to discuss and argue about the language of God and thus to make the religious language intersubjective. This openness made the Christian faith the common cultural good and provided theology with the possibility to exchange the cultural foundation of man's being with other cultural traditions.

Christianity began this cultural exchange in its first centuries and reached the peak in the 13th century. We must bear in mind that this was the time when the first universities were founded. This cultural heritage, the Christian cultural background, which has built the western form of life, was the necessary condition for the exchange of different languages in the first place. It made it possible to pose the question of the relation between faith and science in the western culture. Even all criticism regarding this problem is based on this historical supposition. This question has so far not appeared in the cultures of India or China.

The man as a symbolic being – he experiences the world indirectly

Freedom is an integral part of man, because of it man is a symbolic being (Cassirer 1974). He expresses his world in symbolic terms and can reach the reality only by means of the symbolic; man's world is symbolic in its entirety. Every object, even a scientific one, is a symbolic object. With other words – man can reach only that which is symbolically conveyed.

A mother enables her child to communicate in the symbolic forms of human behaviour, to participate in the human society and to overcome nature. The examples of children brought up by animals show us that man cannot survive as such if he cannot share the first years of his life with a human community. A child must be taught by others (a community), otherwise he/she cannot develop symbolic capacities and lacks the foundation for human identity. Man's ability to survive can be developed only through dialogue between human beings. Man needs other people, through dialogue he develops the ability to govern himself, his body and nature. To be precise – he develops the ability to govern himself and the world through other persons. On one hand he learns to be independent from others, on the other he tries to be connected with people. Human nature is thus not based on an individual person but on the mankind as such: "Culture and social structure impinge on individuals through their subjective interpretation. A major social psychological contribution on this area is its insistence that the linkages between personality and social structure must involve processes that include the individual's perceptions of the social environment (Pettigrew 1997, 432).

Man does not do anything that has not been accepted by his symbolical capacity, which is culturally grounded. Her/his symbolical predispositions make a human being capable to trust and to accept the world, psychologists call it basic trust. We have the union of a mother and her child on one side, and the necessity to overcome this union on the other, because a child should developed his/ her own self, which is his/her primary symbolic experience. His/her experience of an integral relation to his/her mother and at the same sense the possibility to overcome it with her help and build his/her own self enables child's trustful acceptance of reality. A child can experience loneliness and overcome this union with the mother to reach a new, brighter and more fundamental union. According to Winnicott, this is the basis of experiencing a deeper (overpersonal) reality. In this way a child acquires the ability to "trust in advance", which is the basis of a good life and the condition for the religious experience (Winnicott 1951). This much or less satisfying experience accompanies human beings throughout life (Gerjolj 2006), it determines their later relations – it can either secure or prevent good marital relations. (Slatinek 2005) It is probably the first fundamental symbolic experience of man, so all subsequent experiences are influenced by this first fundamental one. Through dialogue man enables himself to communicate: "Interdisciplinary discourse then, is an attempt to bring together disciplines or reasoning strategies that have widely different points or reference, different epistemological foci, and different experimental resources." (Huyssteen 2006, 9)

Consequently, even the scientific language is a symbolic one. This means that all scientific endeavours of the last centuries have been carried out through man's symbolic capacity. His whole existence is an existence transcending itself and can not be the 'object' of anybody's science. This means man's self and all his objects cannot be described without terms, without the language which is a common language of man. Man expresses his experiences, yet these experiences differ between science and faith, as Wittgenstein (1976, 163 - Nr. 6. 432) points out. But all (sc.

experiences) of them are man's experiences and they are grounded in his language.

In the introduction to his *Logik*, Immanuel Kant poses four fundamental questions of philosophy in a cosmopolitan manner. "What can I know? What do I need to do? What can I hope for? What is a person?" According to Kant, the first question is answered by metaphysics, the second by morality, the third by religion and the fourth by anthropology. But Kant argues that all of them (which means everything man can do) can essentially be based on anthropology, since the first three questions are implied in the fourth (Kant 1958, A 25). According to Kant, man's fundamental problems are of practical nature, they can be adequately solved by practical reason. It is practical reason which provides religion, science and ethics with a common concept of man.

As a symbolic being, man has to solve the problem through his language. So he himself is the regulator of his view of the world and also of all his deeds. Language as a universal symbol is the practical framework to organize life and to regulate or overcome details of life as well as the life as a whole. The question of man is therefore the point where metaphysical, ethical, religious and scientific questions meet, not in the way in which anthropology absorbs and replaces other disciplines, but through the basic anthropological perspective in which metaphysical, ethical and religious questions can be studied from a philosophical point of view. With Kant's words: With all scientific questions we have to suppose we are beings with free will, our world is open and our (scientific) world is not the "ultimate one". Scientists of the last centuries (the 19th and 20th) thus tried to reduce scientific questions on the empirical ground in order to avoid this question.

"The need for accountability to our experience also reveals another important epistemological overlap between theological and scientific modes of inquiry. Because we relate to our world epistemicaly only through the mediation of interpreted experience, it may be said that our diverse theologies, and also the sciences, offer alternative interpretations of our experience (Rolston 1987, 1-8). Alternative, however, not in the sense of competing or conflicting interpretations, but of complementary interpretations of the manifold dimensions of our experience." (Huyssteen 2006, 15)

Science is therefore only a part of the framework of man's symbolic world and entails the same practical issue: How can man organize his life better. But this depends on his valuations, his hopes and his strivings. Science is an (important) part of these organisations, especially in the modern world, but it should be always regarded only as a part of the symbolic structure of the world of man. The question of man is thus the question of his symbolic language; it is complex and accompanies the basic decisions of man. Even in this area man cannot act without religious and ethical backgrounds.

Limits of the (symbolic) language

Contemporary Americans and contemporary Europeans as well, seek contradictory goals. They are increasingly distrustful of any authority, political or moral, that would constrain their freedom of choice, but they also want a sense of community and the good things that flow from community, like mutual recognition, participation, belonging, and identity. Community has to be found elsewhere, in smaller and more flexible groups and organisations where loyalties and memberships can be overlapping, and where entry and exit entail relatively low costs. People might thus be able to reconcile their contradictory desires for community and autonomy. But in this bargain, the community they get is smaller and weaker than most that have existed in the past. Each community shares less with neighbouring ones, and the ones to which they belong have relatively little hold. Te circle of people they can trust is necessarily narrower. "The essence of the shift in values that is at the center of the Great Disruption is, then, the rise of moral individualism and the consequent miniaturization of community." (Fukuyama 2000, 91)

These absolute tendencies are still present in sciences. They separate their objects and are themselves divergent. It is increasingly difficult to find a universal scientific language. On the other hand sciences present themselves as more and more absolute. "Against this background I have agreed with Haack that our epistemologies, as well as our standards of rationality, are always contextually shaped yet not hopelessly culture bound." (Hack 1995, 222; Heyssteen 2006,13)

Man as a symbolic being is constantly determined by these so far existing settled cultural patterns, which he accepts as he grows. While the Greeks and people of Middle Ages maintained certain cultural consistency, the subjectivity of modern times opened wide the doors for the subject's gaze and brought into the old monolithic unity the variety established by subjective starting points. This is the beginning of the modern era, the era characterised by the end of metaphysics and by the affirmation of the subject as an entity who autonomously reconstructs the world (Descartes: *cogito, ergo sum*) along with its antagonisms. (Vattimo 1997, 40ff.)

Pascal perceives this as the greatness and misery of mankind (Pascal 2012; Nr. 397-8), which according to Paul Valery lead into the "crisis of spirit". While the world was originally (according to Plato) governed by the concept of the Good (Plato 2013, VI/19), to which every soul must submit and which comes from heaven, that dominated the ancient Greek and medieval world, modernity transposed conceptual (or ideological) management of the world to the earth, thus bestowing divine dimensions in the earthly. That is why modern ideologies tried to appropriate the seal of sacredness.

The Greeks understood language as an activity, as a condition of all others activities (Kamlah 1973, 43). Through language man manages his experiences of life. The problem is that man's life cannot be put under total linguistic control. Man is not able to put the whole life and its experiences into a perfect order. He can control his social life even less: A. MacIntyre is sure that "our social order is in a very literal sense out of our, and indeed anyone's control." (MacIntyre 1986, 107) In his book *Reaching for Good* (Žalec 2005) he critically observes this scientific view of modern bureaucratic lifestyle. It is the problem of modern "positivism, the hegemonic philosophy of the second half of the 19th century", which influenced the thinking of the 20th century (Vattimo 2004,13). The modern thinking was declared objective and neutral, not subjective. But the truth is the opposite, as Žalec points out, quoting Nietzsche, who saw that "what was shown as an objective was in fact a subjective will." (Žalec 2005, 128)

This symbolic language is conditioned by the dialogue with other people and is open to the common search for the whole. Due to the scientific and imperialistic tendencies in the modern culture and in the scientific and cultural (especially political) patterns, the language is going rapidly towards totalisation, which was what Wittgenstein focused on. He stressed that we can act, but we cannot make theories of our actions. With other words – man's actions are (practically) legitimated by his making decisions. They are legitimated games among other games in language, yet they are not legitimated as a 'last' or 'special' or 'ultimate' or 'not-provable' games. This is valid for all games of languages. As Hans Kraml pointed out, is it very important to have the possibility to play different games, to analyse and to criticise them. Without this we cannot decide the validity of games within the entire context of man's language, since man has the ability not only to speak but also to set the rules of speaking. These games should be exchangeable and compatible (Kraml 1984, 71). The basic characteristic of man is dialogue. "What Nickolas Rescher (1993, 3f) called *dissensus tolerance* will prove to be a positive and constructive part of pluralism in theology and science dialogue. It is at this point that we reach beyond our specific traditions in crosscontextual conversation to a shared wide reflective equilibrium where the diversity of our traditions will yield the diversity of our experiences, the diversity of our epistemic situations, the diversities of our epistemic situations, the diversities of our values and methodologies. In theology and science dialogue, the most sensible posture is therefore to accept the reality of cognitive pluralism." (Heyssteen 2006, 33)

Man is growing up in this symbolic world through dialogue, which is the basic property of language. All games of languages throughout man's life and all his occupations can be performed only in dialogue (Vattimo 2004, 51, 79ff.). This can be observed especially during early years of one's life. A child can speak only through other people. He comes to himself through others. Charles Taylor says: "Human beings are self-interpreting animals." (Taylor 1985, 45) There are no objective languages without subjective suppositions and dialogue.

Taylor's interpreter, Walter Schaupp, points out that according to Taylor man is "a subject of systems of sense, meaning, symbols." (Schaupp 2003, 154) Man is interpreting the whole world in symbolic terms. Science is also a product of his symbolic ability. Bertrand Russell claims: "Philosophy should show us the hierarchy of our instinctive beliefs, beginning with those we hold most strongly, and presenting each as much isolated and as free from irrelevant additions as possible. It should take care to show that, in the form in which they are finally set forth, our instinctive beliefs do not clash, but form a harmonious system. There can never be any reason for rejecting one instinctive belief except that it clashes with others; thus, if they are found to harmonize, the whole system becomes worthy of acceptance." (Russel 1980, 12) As the modern world appears in its aporias, the system of language should be proved, many thinkers of the 20th century contemplated this problem of modern scientific culture. Jürgen Habermas and Karl Otto Apel are criticizing, for example, the totalitarisation of the political, economical and technical systems. (Vattimo 2004, 83)

"Facts" and the "perfection of science"

Owen Flanagan analyzes the problem of 'psychological facts' in the moral knowledge. He comes to the following conclusions: "First, a theory with the structure of Kantianism or utilitarianism will need to inculcate not only its own abstract decision procedure but also certain recognitial skills for perceiving problems which deserve the application on that decision procedure. It is extremely unlikely one could become proficient at recognizing moral challenges as defined by the lights of such a conception without its changing the way the world is *seen*. Second, once things are understood in this way, it is easy to recognize that an abstraction charge which is first levelled at a particular decision procedure on the grounds that it factors out too much (or too little) might also be levelled against the modes of moral perception and the methods of individuating moral challenges which the theory engenders." (Flanagan 1991, 87)

These examples from psychology or ethics show us that the problem of 'facts' in all sciences is not easy to solve. Our knowledge is always an abstraction and every abstraction is levelling. With other words - all empirical knowledge is contingent on the view of a spectator. So research is not neutral and without values. It is impossible to observe the fundamental norms of scientists, which "are mainly honesty, objectivity, tolerance, doubt of certitude and unselfish engagement." (Cournand 1977, 700) Scientists are conditioned by their 'world view', their theoretical and ideological suppositions: "Empirical knowledge is notoriously theory-laden, subject to various interpretations, and is easy to mistake truths *about local* (stressed by J. Juhant), socially specific features of persons for deep facts about our natures. Indeed, continuous revision is, in one sense, a permanent feature of this project. This is not only because the project of naturalizing ethics is in its early stages, and because psychology is still a young science. It is also due to the fact that truly naturalistic ethics tracks, and engages in critical reflection on, social changes, which themselves bring about changes in our natures. We know that such changes are inevitable. But we can have little knowledge in advance of the forms they will take." (Flanagan 1991, 333)

The last centuries were markedly ideological and totalitarian. The totalitarisation of language and of the entire culture came with scientism. Auguste Comte declared the scientific era or set the scientific norm. All questions of man's life should be solved by science. The methodology includes measuring, empirical proving and establishing facts. How can one get facts and how many facts are there? Is man's life a fact among other facts? How can facts be explained if man is "an open project" and all questions are influenced by his symbolical ability? The philosophies of the 20th century tried to find the formula for declaring or defining facts. The so-called Vienna Circle began very influential discussions. They asked: „How the sentences and theories are to be tested?" (Zelger 1989, 50) The members of the Vienna Circle tried to find the possible sentences which could be proved through experience. "Raw and pure facts" according to this view then seem to be singular events, states, or states of affairs, the *hic et nunc* of Aristotelian metaphysics. Such an interpretation invites comparison with Wittgenstein's *Tractatus*. For there sentences are pictures of thoughts and these in turn are pictures of facts. Surely Witgenstein's concept of facts could be interpreted in such a way that also general facts, like natural laws, become possibly pictured. But the essential point of Wittgenstein's conception is that "the world consists of elementary facts which are depicted by elementary sentences." (Zelger 1989, 51)

Wittgenstein himself is a good example for the dilemmas concerning the limitation of the scientific language. In *Tractatus*, even he is convinced about the facts of reality, he speaks about the mysticism of reality. Because of this he later tried to find the solution in the games of language. The solution for the scientific and the religious language can be found. He was in fact very throughout his life concerned about religious question. For him the mysticism of the world derives from its very existence, not from the question about the manner of its existence (Wittgenstein 1976; Nr. 6. 44). In this sense the next phrase of *Tractatus* is very important: "*Das Gefühl der Welt als begrenztes Ganzes ist das Mystische*"– "the feeling of the world as a limited wholeness is the mysticism." (6.45) This seems to confirm that all (scientific) phrasings of the word are limited. With other words – facts cannot be the 'last words' of the world. This should not be understood only in the sense that facts are not the ultimate reality but also that facts are not the whole reality. "From the consciousness of the oneness of my life is coming out the religion-science - and art." (Wittgenstein 1963, 171) Wittgenstein is also the author of the famous sentence saying that one could not play the game of language alone. Quoting this phrase, Otto Apel stresses that we always need the rules of language, even when we are trying to make a new language. It means that makers of the scientific language depend in their endeavours on the universal base of language which is used in their communities (Vattimo 2004, 82). In the same sense Karl Popper says that a dictator depends on the opinion of his citizens. In other words – he cannot play his tyrant game without his subjects. In the same way one alone cannot play his game of language. In this sense totalitarisation of language could be overcome through dialogue.

Life is a wholeness, it is not just a part or a fragment of our world. We are also involved in the whole human community. We share the community with other people; it is the basis of all our actions, because we play our games of language together. Even scientific, political and economical games are played on the common basis of our language. Nobody has his own language; any language is always the language we all share: scientists, seekers of God, sceptics. Nobody has the monopoly of a language. Contrary to this, modern systems have tried to install the total closed lingual order.

Totalisation of thinking is absolutisation of parts of the reality

Kenneth Gergen is criticizing the totalisation of thinking in modern times because it has entrenched its positions and excluded others so as to destroy them. Religion was thus expelled from the curricula of universities and replaced by science (Gregen 1996, 397).

Not only do such systems truncate, oppress, and obliterate alternative forms of social lives, they also exclude others. This is the problem of modern totalitarian systems: communism, various extreme nationalisms (Fascism, Nazism, etc.). The problem is that totalitarian systems are not willing to accept any options that differ from theirs. Even more, they turn the particular into the absolute and they do not allow any other possibilities. Marxists made absolute statements and thus suppressed any dialogue. The same tendencies are present in different segments of modern society. The process of production supported by media tries to exclude all other possible options and unite the world of production. Language will be increasingly universalised and univocal. It is not an accident that the whole world uses the English language. The "lingua franca" is the technical equipment to universalize the world and to suspend the particular experiences.

The study of the mediaeval thinking shows that – opposite to common opinion – the mediaeval thinkers persist on the plurality, and the modern times with the absolutisations of the particular experiences only brought the problems of the total thinking (Flasch 2000, 351-362). In the same manner catholic thinkers tried to preserve the unity of the scholastic world, "the beautiful, splenid times", but it disappeared fast or it was replaced by the scientific world: "Es waren schöne glänzende Zeiten, wo Europa ein christliches Land war, wo Eine Christenheit diesen menschlich gestalteten Weltteil beiwohnte; ein großes gemeinschaftliches Interesse verband die entlegensten Provinzen dieses christlichen Reichs." (Novalis 1963, 37)

Comte and Hegel (each in his own manner) tried to replace this Christian world with the scientific world. The opinion spread that our world is a scientific one. Contrary to this and to oppose this scientific totalisation, catholic scholastics built Thomistic scientific world. In both cases faith took a backseat, while science dominated and still dominates in these systems. By striving for the Novalis' reign of Christendom, Catholic scholastics built their scientific faith to level the ideological status of the scientific language.

It is man's anthropological need to search the wholeness of his worldview and to turn his world to a global unity. Man living in the uterus of his mother is striving to retain this open world as a closed wholeness. It is man's primary necessity to have a closed world. Sloterdijk is quoting Hans Blummenberg: "The polis is repeatedness of the cave (the uterus) with other means." (Sloterdijk 1999, 151) According to Winnicott, however, man has to grow up and find otherness and thus come to a transcendent, religious perspective of life. It could be reached only if a mother opens herself and leave her child to others. In this way a child is opening her/himself to a deeper reality transcending the interpersonal relations, which is the condition for this deeper experience of faith.

But the modern scientific world is dismissing the personal world. Even more – technical and scientific organisation of the world creates an ever increasing gap between the scientific and the personal world. One can easily notice the ubiquitous tendencies to uniform this world and to subject the personal world to the scientific-technical world and thus close it. That is why Marxists did not tolerate any personal opinion: all the world for everybody is an ideological system. People should be regarded as immature, as children. These tendencies can be seen today in the so-called "world of productions". One is not allowed to be a grown-up person, to make personal decisions or to express his/her own needs, all this have to be subjected to the system of production and media. Man is reduced to a mere function in these media-technical processes.

This process, which began with the scientism, came to the perfection in modern times with the processes of economical and technical globalisation. There is no place for man and his own personal world; he has to satisfy the technical and economic needs of systems. In this closed world there is no place for desires and beliefs. There is no place for dialogue between people, not even for the dialogue with God. Language is reduced to a function of the system. Good examples of this are communist systems.

France is a scene of these conflicts and struggles as it is the cradle of modern revolutions and all that they entailed. French thinkers are also a prototype of the struggles in a modern society. The first French revolution officially replaced the worship of God with the worship of mind during Danton's dictatorship. This was a worship of the scientific mind and a worship of the exclusiveness. Pascal's said the New Age man, who was beginning to stand on his own feet, experienced his highness and also his misery (Pascal 1986, 53ff.); we now see its consequences. French thinkers of the time were the prototype of the strife between the traditional Christendom and the pugnacious unfaith, between the radical revolutionaries and the traditional compromisers, between searching and risk on one side, and the conservative ossification on the other.

The problem of God was the crucial question in all this struggles. Already Pascal reproached Descartes for harnessing God to the cart of his rational system (Pascal 1986, 60). God got his rational place in the whole system and he was no longer God. This project of the New Ages went its own ways and it is also understandable that all revolutionary praxis became religious and prophetical, they became divine (Guiton 1970, 249).

Dialogue: Faith and science – the world and God

All our discussion opens the basic dilemma which accompanies the entire Christian culture in its relation to the modern period. According to the teaching of Thomas Aquinas and his followers, as well as according to the teaching of the Catholic Church, there is no antagonism between faith and science; philosophy could be used to strengthen faith (Leon 1879, in: DS Nr. 3135-3140). According to the Church's tradition, faith and reason supplement each other since they are both derived from God.

But scholastics could not easily understand the modern process which began with the Enlightenment and which Ernst Cassirer calls a "secularisation". The concept in quotation marks has a wider meaning and denotes a disruption: modern thinkers no longer recognise God as the link binding the whole world; this worldview was in decline. Consequently, there is also no more unity between the scientific world and the personal world, between God and man. But modern thinkers and scientists build their knowledge on a new, reduced yet total worldview, the so-called scientific worldview; the so-called "objective" science is becoming a worldview. In this sense is "Szientismus also der *Glaube* an die vollständige wissenschaftliche Erklärbarkeit der Natur … Das kann soweit gehen, dass die Kompetenz der Wissenschaft für die Beurteilung der *gesamten Lebenswelt* der Menschen in Anspruch genommen wird bis hin zu Entwürfen für die "wissenschaftliche" Gesellschaftsordnung z. B. sozialistischer oder nationalsozialistischer Prägung" ("scientism is the belief in the perfect scientific explanation of nature." (Gelhaus 2006, 95) This picture of science is completely depersonalised and it does not acknowledge any criteria of a subject, which are involved in all actions and processes of man.

Modern Christian thinkers in different (especially European) countries are trying to find solutions to these fundamental dilemmas. Some appeared at the end of 19th and at the beginning of the 20th century: Bergson, Blondel, Breher, Maritain, Rahner, Jaspers, Gadamer, Kocbek, Truhlar etc.

As we have seen, belief, valuation and judgment cannot be separated from man's activities; on the contrary, they are their substratum. Consequently, man has to deal with the grounds of his existence, which have a common mystical ground and cannot be analytically expressed. Man displays an invincible hope, sovereignty and ability to unify all his activities. But this unification cannot be a technical or neoscholastic "objective" world.

As Karl Löwith stresses in his book *The Meaning in History* (1949), the modern time could not replace the Biblical-Christian idea of Kingdom of God with the secularized idea of the progress or any other idea like this. It is also difficult to find the solution on the intersubjective basis as Jürgen Habermas in *Glauben und Wissen* (2001) points out, especially because of the tendencies in modern thought to declare the religion as irrational. But it is inconsequent to exclude the last question of man even in the scientific era. According to J. Guitton, the modernistic critique tried to expel the 'surnatural' from religion. Could the rational criteria for the language of God be found? If, according to Muck, "the sentences about God could be logically analyzed", (Muck 1999, 20) how can the religious language survive this exclusive scientific situation? The modern media and technical world are not willing to renounce the excluding tendencies, which make man's needs for the meaning, for the moral sense and for mystical grounds superfluous. But there is not only one language, because any language depends on different human suppositions, evaluations and also on different communities. There are also different scientific communities:

"Scientists who treat the issue of human uniqueness as if it were only a biological or anthropological event, and theologians who threat it as only a spiritual or religious issue, want the book of human nature to be written in only one language. No one disciplinary language, however, can ever completely capture every aspect of the complex issue we are trying to understand here, and this will become an important argument against those disciplinary purists who are made uneasy by the messiness of multiple vocabularies in interdisciplinary research." (Huyssteen 2006, 35/36) This is important in all other aspects of scientific work.

There is a new belief, a 'common sense', which intervenes not only in the public sphere but is determining the personal lives of all people on this earth. This replaced all what used to be the domain of man's religious life or what was determined as the meaning of life by the Catholic Church before. Today the breviary is replaced by TV or electronic news, religious liturgy by media or a shopping spree in supermarkets. According to Marshall McLuhan and Paul Virilio, man's perception of the world is today determined by electronic mediators (McLuhan 1967; Virilio 1988). Man is a symbolic being, so this mediation has a new symbolic language

– the symbolic of medium (Juhant 2006). His world is created by the schemes which are planned by the theorists of media. Even the democratic society is in this way regulated from above and displays totalitarian trends. This tendencies to regard man as a machine will be increased by the biotechnical industry. A universalized mediated belief is a new ideology.

It is understandable that philosophers will be more and more critical of these ideologisations of language. It is the imperative of the moment to liberate man of the machine (Mumford, Maritain), man of the celerity (Virilio), man of media (McLuhan) and man of the modern violence (Girard).

The attempts of neoscholastics offered a bad solution, they tried to give a local answer (from a single point of view) and to restore the (classical) religious world. This world is gone. It is marked by openness to a difficult situation of (post)modern man and readiness for dialogue, openness for different points of view, for a common search in order to answer these questions. It is an ethical task, since it will take all man's sources to escape from the labyrinth into which he plunged. The manner in which our society functions do not allow taking time for dialogue, not even in childhood.

The result is that a mother cannot introduce her child to the natural dialogical basis of a symbolic language, and later a child has to make do with religious surrogates. A child cannot be enabled to avoid his hermetically closed lingual situation and he/she will be later predisposed to dependence and also to one-sidedness and obedience to totalitarianism.

In our liberalistic times it comes as no surprise that man's experiences are limited by the individualistic 'earthly' dimensions and not open to the common sense, which can be exercised and reached only by lingual means and dialogue, which is limited in advance. But who will enable him for this job? Man cannot live without a belief, the problem is how to recognize his fundamental openness and to express it in dialogue and to build a cultural integrated symbolic world with others.

It is not possible to limit this problem only by mystical experience – even mysticism has a language, although this language has to be reached through the theological language, which conveys the religious mystical experience to others. One can progress only if he/she is enabled in dialogical language, basically he must be prepared to accept her/his points of view as limited and to recognize others as partners in dialogue. As we have seen at Winnicott, a child should in the first days on this earth learn to be open for the otherness and will thus be prepared to take part in dialogical situations and be open for the Otherness, which means for God.

The man cannot find himself without this truth regarding human existence today. J. Guitton stresses the importance of philosophy in relation to faith, yet he is convinced that the basis of the Christian faith is love, which was made known through Jesus Christ on the Cross (Guitton 1992, 106ff.). Love is the basis of man, but we must ask how man can reach this experience if he lives in a non-personal world. This is the question of our Christian communities or our Christian testimony of Christ's Love (Juhant 2005). Yet it is also the question of human community as a whole. According to Guitton, the Christian belief is despite this a wholeness combining reason, faith, experience and history.

Disruption: Ethics as a link between science and faith

We have found that the total modern systems cannot adequately solve the problem of faith. On the contrary – the modern systems have prevented man to experience the limitedness of this world: its political, economical or media view. It is just a limited worldview aspiring for the openness which is possible only through a dialogical worldview. It is impossible to come to faith without the dialogue with other people – the process which begins in the first years of human life. It implies that an individual must get the basic experience of love and at the same time experiences of his dialogical position in the world.

So there are no systematic solutions to the question of the relation between science and faith. That does not mean that we do not have any logical materials for this task, this task is a practical one and can be performed within a lingual and dialogical community, it cannot be done objectively, neutrally and without being there in person. It is valuable for all human activities. F. Grinnell points out: "The scientific attitude itself is a potential source of ethical problems when this attitude is transformed in a secular faith." (Grinell 1992, 139) It implies the decision, and every scientist, theologian or philosopher searches for the truth in dialogue.

With other words – a mother gives her child love, thus certainty and safety, she opens the world of language and leads her child into it. She also introduces him/her to the world of dialogue and helps him/her to overcome the unbearable aloneness. A child also learns to accept the fundamental grounds of life: himself (soul), the material world (his/her mother and other people who give him safety and possibilities to be open for the otherness and God (religious openness). So a child will be enabled to experience the openness of our language and to take an opportunity to overcome this aloneness in a practical dialogue (Winnicott 1951). A child can live for a short time with surrogates (games, television and other comforters), but he/she always needs a personal contact to find a solution in this position. The up-till-now experiences determine the next dialogue – a practical issue.

In this way all our experiences need other person. Even scientists owe their capacity to work and have dialogues in their daily lives and also in their scientific practice to this fundamental experience with their parents, teachers and other persons. If this dialogical procedure does not work, clashes appear. All languages should also be open enough for the deeper and especially for the long-term aspect of life. It takes a living dialogue to come together in different languages and to open new perspectives (Huyssteen 2006, 32ff.).

We cannot restore the old classical system to solve the problems of people's belief today. Science cannot replace theology nor can theology restore the total religious system. Neither theology nor science can denounce their specific languages. In the postmodern era we are much more invited to practice dialogue. When compared with the time of Thomas Aquinas, we are in a much more difficult situation; even he had this experience in 13th century. We have to combine different languages: those of different sciences, that of media, the language of the economically globalised world and so on. If man undergoes the primary experience of the basis which sustains him and if is thus convinced that this acknowledgment of God's love enables him to live in accordance to this, he will through acknowledging others make this dialogue possible. This is a personal-ethical task. If we are convinced that God acknowledged us, we are fit for the acknowledgement of others.

According to Winnicott, Bauman and Vetlessen, it is this personal experience whose consequence is the ethical decision to acknowledge others. Only a person with this primary experience can give this experience to others. There is no job for the system, as Zygmund Bauman points out, only the person can do it. In this sense an individual person is the basis for the solution of man's questions. According to Bauman, systems are interested only in solving the problems of the system (Bauman 1995).

If the best praxis is a good theory, than a good theory of belief is a communicable one, which prepares us for the exchange with (different) others. The same holds true for a scientific theory or philosophy. In this sense the problem of relation between philosophy, science and faith is an ethical one. If a person is open enough to other persons, persons will overcome the limitedness of their systems and find in dialogue the solutions which would not exclude others.

According to Levinas and Bauman, the person is a mirror of man. We should see man as otherness, as a condition of our survival, because for man the ethical responsibility is the ground for the survival of man as such. It is also the ground for cooperating and building a community. There is, however, a difference between the claim of Levinas and Bauman to take the Other as a Face, on one side, and God's gentleness towards man, on the other. Because man experiences the love of God, he can respond with his love. For Christianity this is not ethics but theology, since God came forward and acknowledged man, thus giving us the basis for acting ethically (Knapp 2006, 206ff.). In this sense we can regard Kant's postulates – the Soul, the World, and God – as conditions for man's practical life, not only in the religion but also in the daily life in the science, each time for different reasons: in philosophy it is the ethical postulate of the Otherness (as a Face), while in theology it is God's love towards man. Because of it the Christian belief is ethics, yet not ethics alone, because God's love is the basic religious experience of man: he was acknowledged and named through God's love and he can also respond to this love. It is the basis for the possibility to love (Žalec 2005, 175ff.) and to build a Christian community.

There is no faith without a loving community, a community which acknowledges others. It is also the ground for the possibility to acknowledge the Otherness – a possibility to find in it the place for God. It this sense theology, philosophy and science can be compared: all three are tested whether they are willing to acknowledge the otherness. Man as a person is in this sense always a moral person or represents an obligation which should be accepted and respected in all circumstances (Ricken 2006, 71).

It is therefore a postulate of science, philosophy, theology and daily life experience. It supposes a dialogue in all complicated human activities, including scientific ones. It is chiefly a philosophical problem, yet also a theological one and a problem of science, the problem of openness of their languages. It affects not only the Christian community but the whole human community. We are increasingly pressed to solve this question in the openness of our languages and in the readiness to hear each other out, to communicate with others. This communication should be particularly careful not to exclude the weak: embryos, the elderly and the poor, as well as other parts of the society. We should not give up speaking as long as we can speak.

We have to discuss this problem in the competent philosophical, religious (theological) and scientific communities. Because it is at least the question of morality, we have to speak about this in the whole human (globalised) community. Are we prepared to make room for other persons? This is the "To be or not to be" of the globalised world we are living in and in which we are much more oriented towards each other. The openness for others could be reached through the openness for the Other, for the unlimited love. This is a practical question of our faiths. It cannot be determined, yet we can acknowledge that human life has this openness and that this openness makes man free. According to Levinas, man is free if he acknowledges the otherness, because he was (before) acknowledged by God. Philosophy, theology and all sciences have to practice this openness and be aware of the human mystery through constant dialogue.

5. LIVING WITH(IN) DIALOGUE - PATH TO THE ART OF A (GOOD) PERSONAL AND SOCIAL LIFE

The clash of civilizations as a menace

The development of modern society is about to encounter serious problems, apart from the fact that "the clashes of civilizations" are intensifying. Some serious questions have emerged: will be there enough resources for the survival of the coming generations? Will people who have enough to eat be ready to share the existing food supply? And how will future generations live? We have already problems with the emissions of CO_2 and there is a growing problem of pollution. How to provide the sources of energy, water and other necessary resources for the survival of all men?

There are still clashes between peoples about the manner of distributing the present supply of essential raw materials, sources of energy and water. The wars or oppression in Tibet and Rwanda, the conflicts between Russia and other states of the former Soviet Union, especially with the NATO allies, between South and North Korea, Japan and China, and other South-East Asian countries, between Iran and other Islamic states and Israel stem from the difficult task of finding a language of cooperation which would enable sharing of goods among all people. The dispute between Slovenia and Croatia, two relatively small countries, is about the redistribution of economical power gained by traffic ways in the Adriatic Sea.

The main problem is the lack of dialogue on these questions. All partners lack the willingness to train in the ways of dialogue. There are many reasons behind this. The liberal thinking as a basis of the modern production system does not take care for underprivileged groups. Particularly children, women, and powerless people in general are excluded from the process of dialogue. They are not able to participate in these modern processes on equal grounds. As John Rawls pointed out, there should be equal positions for all people and everybody should have general access to the main societal positions and sources. But differences in the so-called global world make it difficult to provide everybody with an equal starting point (Rawls 1999). The liberal manner of the Darwinian paradigm encourages the exclusion and rivalry, and it seems to be the predominant mode of the political, economic and other societal life as such. This, however, promotes exclusion of the weak. So the prevailing formula of modern life is not cooperation but exclusion.

The modern liberalistic way of life, the ways of negotiation in the politics and in other individual and societal areas of human endeavour do not address real problems of being, nor promote dialogue, because the tendencies of protectionism, exclusion and discriminations prevail. Yet the global development demands dialogue and cooperation. It seems there is no other way than a living dialogue about the civic and cultural foundations of our development.

The "lack of feelings"

Cooperation and dialogue must be learnt. Young people should be introduced to dialogue in order to experience their human being and to learn to deal with it. If these prerequisites of free dialogue in lives of families and other basic structures of society are not granted, man cannot develop his human capacities to live as a human being.

How can man develop the ability for dialogic communication? This happens mostly in the first years of one's life. If children grew up among animals they could not develop any of these foundations of human life. Similarly, children growing up in dysfunctional or asocial families experience difficulties in contacts with others. The modern way of life provides children with few or no possibilities to socialise with their parents or other relational persons. They are predominantly using non-living means of communications – electronic media and internet – their abilities for genuine human communication is thus stunned. Consequently, young people are unable to deal with their feelings, though this is a sine qua non for normal human communication. They cannot be consistently familiarised with the main elements of human being and they are weak or incapable to perform any inter-human exchange. If they are not enabled to develop their first emotional life, they will not be able to mend it later.

The popularity of talk-shows, therapeutic workshops and other communication services comes as no surprise, as they are trying to compensate for this serious human deficiency in modern society. Because of this marriages are not stable, young people are not capable of a steady living dialogue nor can they share their problems. The same holds true in other areas of life.

Who will enable man in his human condition and teach him the way of dialogue? In modern non-personal relations parents and relational persons lack time and opportunities to enable their children to learn the forms of dialogue. Most of our daily life is enacted only through business and other impersonal activities. The "lack of feeling" is compensated by searching for special events, "full adventures", "enriched" by alcohol, drugs and sexual exploits, all of which are a way to compensate for the lack of feelings exchange. These all are consequences of the modern competitive and excluding society.

Criticising this "one-sided way" society, Joachim Bauer, in his book *Prinzip Menschlichkeit* (A Principle of Humanity 2006) denounces Darwin's "war of nature" as a principle of inhumanity. Darwin's notion that man and the entire nature are inherently determined to struggle for life, and that this struggle means war of all against all, is not in accordance with human nature, it is indoctrinated. Yet this is exactly how Richard Dawkins (2006) revives Darwinism by stressing that the "selfish gene" directs our actions. Bauer stresses that life is enabled by cooperation, while Darwin and Dawkins ignore this fact of life. They maintain that in Western culture struggle and fight prevailed over cooperation and connectedness. According to Bauer, we can find ample examples of this cooperation in nature, as well as in our own lives. Bauer points out: "The model of Darwin neglects the fundamental characteristic of phenomena which stays at the beginning of all biology, the phenomenon of the cooperation." (Bauer 2006, 128)

The process of dialogue as a condition for a good life

Joachim Bauer considers man a being of dialogue. He is of the opinion that human genes are predisposed to cooperation and not struggle. The man is by his nature predisposed to cooperate and not to exclude others. There are no proofs that human genes are by nature made to exclude others. On the contrary: Bauer as a physician confirms that genes are willing to cooperate. Aggression is caused by lack of cooperation and love. Cooperation is so important for us that, as Bauer stresses, our brains do not agree with uncooperative unfairness; they consider such behaviour punishable (Bauer 2006, 185).

Life of nature and man is according Bauer to a large extent cooperation and not exclusion, it means that man is willing to cooperate and not to fight. This view of dialogic life seems to oppose the way Rene Girard regards the genesis of life. He emphasises that from the beginning of human civilization the struggle of all against all seems to be the prevailing mode of existence, and modern society also confirms this.

The scapegoat

Rene Girard is dealing with desiring and phenomenon of malice as a crucial problem of all societies. As we know, for Buddhists desires are the cause of malice.

Man desires objects because others possess them. To get objects means to compete with others who own them. The primary objects of desire are food, territory and women (Palaver 2003, 69). This desire for possession stimulates the one who desires to imitate (*mimesis*) his rival with the objects of his desire. This is, according to Girard, the main characteristic of individuals and groups. This can be easily seen in children. When one child is playing with a toy or a tool, the other will want to play with the same toy or tool. The same struggle occurs between families, groups, nations. All this should follow strict and exact societal rules. When a crisis erupts due to scarcity of goods, members of a society have to search for solutions to avoid clashes or wars.

Girard, like Thomas Hobbes, is convinced there is some "natural violent condition". It is the state of war, all against all. This is the mimetic crisis (Girard: *fureur mimétique*, *emballement mimétique*, *effervescence collective*). The cultural history knows different examples of this crisis and the culture is in fact a way of dealing with these crises or, which is the same, a way such crises could be solved. Different societies worked out precise mechanisms to deal with these societal situations, which are in some cases very dangerous. People are bound to find the so-called "scapegoat" to overcome a crisis.

According to Girard, there are two principal ways to solve the "mimetic crisis": the first is more usual and present throughout the history of mankind and is described both in ancient myths and modern literature. In times of crisis people find a scapegoat to avoid clashes or war of all against all. Girard speaks about *the mimesis of reunification* or about *the mimesis of reconciliation.* But this could achieved only with a scapegoat. To avoid the mimetic or sacrificial crisis, it is necessary to channel the mimetic desire (Girard 1987, 26).

The other is a Christian solution. Christianity differs from other teachings in that it takes the position of victims. Through Jesus Christ offerings Christians are invited to intercede on behalf of the poor. The so-called "mimetic situation" has to be overcome by willingly accepting the position of the weak.

Nothing without sacrifice

These observations by Joachim Bauer and René Girard, as well as the experiences of our daily lives, help us see the gravity of the mimetic crisis. Modern man was by Darwin's theory and galloping technology pushed into the current competition and rivalry. According to Girard, man as such is always a rival because he desires the objects of his fellowmen. Societies have always encountered the problem of how to overcome this rivalry. The other has been always the standard against which one measures himself. In the same sense the other is one's rival, because he wants to posses the same "things", the same goods, his rival is trying to obtain. Rivalry emerges because goods are limited in quantity. Rivals have to reach a peaceful solution to sustain their societal order and to prevent shortages of goods. Yet this cannot be done without sacrifice.

In modern liberal society the situation changes, especially in the post-communist societies. They display increasing tendencies toward rivalry, ousting the other and taking goods for oneself, societal equidistance is thus weakened. These tendencies are augmented by economist and financial decision-makers. Multinational companies and their owners are gathering ever more economic and financial power, thus ousting the other. The society is consequently divided into the player and the excluded – "the third". The modern society is a quite well adapted society, yet it does not take care of all its members. Involved in the system are the so-called "*double-binds*". Apart from them, there are those who do not participate in societal connections, "the third". The old societies knew only the rivalry between *double-binds*. All conflicts and use of force usually occur between *double-binds*, it means the society consisted only of rivals who have "to solve the problem". They had to act according to the sacrificial or mimetic crisis to preserve the well-adapted society.

According to Girard, the essence of *mimesis* is insincerity, as the society functions with some insincere suppositions. It accepts the covert suppositions of desires and the pertaining rivalry. Insincerity is the basis of new myths referring to these desires. To overcome this insincerity, people should be always aware of their obligations to this mythic past. Against this background, people were in the past always reminded to uphold stable societal relations, it means one should not question this mythical supposition but preserve and to cultivate it. All people in these primordial societies took part in the mimetic sacrificial mystery and were thus all equal. They were obliged to sustain the equivalence of society. Lack of goods was inconceivable as it would have disastrous consequences.

Paul Dumouchel shows how Girard's mimetic theory works in modern global conditions. This society tolerates scarcity of goods but it has also invented the third, the excluded. The societies of old also included rivals, "the principle of solidarity was the anti-mimetic brake." (Dumouchel/Depuy 1999, 234) The mimetic crisis channelled desires to prevent shortages of goods. Desires are nowadays subordinated to "perpetual growth". The members of the global world society are trained to accept economic growth as the solution for all societal problems. But this philosophy (and psychology) could be sustainable only under the condition the world community is prepared to sacrifice its weak members. The excluded are not able to participate in this process. Even more – they are sacrificed for this development. In this "process of perpetual growth" the modern society has been sacrificing ever more victims. Modern systems were built on the supposition that scapegoats were never in short supply, there would be always enough of them. Nazism invented Jews and Slavs, communism could not do without class-enemies. The today's "world-liberalistic" multinational system produces large numbers of homeless powerless children, people living on the street and in overcrowded suburbs. They are not hungry for the lack of food in the world but for the lack of will to expose the insincere suppositions of modern society and to include all people in the world's development.

Here the question arises of how to find in the modern global world positive options, so people would be willing to cooperate and include "the third". Either there is an alternative solution to this problem or we will simply wait for the homeless masses to come to our Shengen border or to other doors, knocking and appealing to our conscience. This means: if we are not willing to cooperate with them and through dialogue solve the main problems of mankind, like the distribution of food, resources and territory, we invite global clashes.

However, solving of sacrifice crises demands willingness to sacrifice. This is human or Christian aspect of the question. Man should not give in to the dead systems but should as a being of dialogue and cooperation find ways to solve these tensions. Yet man is an ambivalent being. He is a rival on one hand and a partner in dialogue on the other – from the anthropo-logical point of view. Whether he is prepared to overcome his natural tendency to rivalry depends on his socialisation and cultural background. Christianity teaches the way of love and empathy and tries to enable man to live this way. Girard is convinced that Christianity is a teaching of the non-violent mimesis ("imitation non violent"- Palaver 2003, 278).

What does it mean? Is the Christian way really a way of man which enables man to become a being of dialogue? If man learns or carries out dialogue, he will empower himself for an authentic human life. This could be reached through feeling and the exchange of human feelings. But how could man overcome the natural egoistic tendency to compete? With other words: how can man solve mimetic crises, especially in case of the modern liberal way of life? Things make us live according to the art of rivalry and grabbing. If modern civilisation is a civilisation of competition, how could one be limited, made ready to give way to the other and be humane? Is it possible to act or live in a society without having to obey and uphold only competitive rules, is it possible to accept the other even though he is not able to take part in this competitive societal game? With the words of Pope Benedict XVI.: Are only the logics of competitive exchange possible or are there the political logics of dialogue and "the logic of unconditional gift", too? (Benedict XVI. 2009, Nr. 37).

The real being

Erich Fromm worked out the importance of being versus having. Fromm enumerates the elements of the genuine being: relatedness, creativity, rootedness, a sense of identity and a frame of orientation (Fromm 2007, 71ff.). This confirms that man's being is deepened in the wholeness of being. We have to attain genuine being. In his expositions about the art of life in Eckhartian way, Dietmar Mieth (2007) says that the way to live for

Master Eckhart was not to life for (worumwillen) but to live ex. The man is fully engaged in living for, in Frommian mode he lives to have. He is working for his purposes but he cannot live from (ex) his grounds. For Master Eckhart life is flowing from the unity of being, and this unity is God. A man who would act in different manner should transform himself: he should act from the inner, not from the outer. To act from the inner, man needs to be open to his inner ground. For Eckhart this inner ground is God. This is the birth of the Son of God in the soul of man.

The real being is a being distanced from appearances. Appearances entangle or blind man. The real life is the life in the real being, which is God. It means that nothing (including people) is final and we have to open to the real being, which is God. Understanding and love open us to this reality. According to Johannes Tauler, to live in love means the real conversion. Love is the only living power; 1 Cor 13, 3: "If I give away all I have, and I deliver my body to be burned, but I have not love, I gain nothing." Love is empathy for the other, it means to be ready for the art of dying (to himself = *ars moriendi*). In the end he has to live without desiring anything, he has to die to everybody and everything.

The Christian way opens us to the real being. This is a prayer, it is a dialogue. We cannot make progress without dialogue with the other (man and God). As childhood experiences show, dialogue opens us to our real being. The experience of a child is the experience of a living dialogue and a living being. This is a dimension of God's kingdom, of full humanity and the source of a real and full life. The way to come to it is always sincere dialogue which does not end at man's borders but remains open for unlimited openness. To come to this stage of development, man needs to pass "the dark night", as mystics said. This "dark night" could be endured by dying to oneself.

Ars moriendi vs. ars of grabbing

Christian thinkers of Middle Ages spoke a lot about the art of dying (*ars moriendi*). They perceived man as a dialectics of rest and motion (Flasch 2000, 185). Man is a mobile being and because of it more of a not-being as a being, as master Eckhart pointed out (Flasch 2000, 266). But "man should renounce the world, the self and God". He should be just moved from life itself. In this sense man is without plans, without systems, without way; his life should be abandoning movement within, becoming still. Such life is a life without works, without honours for your deeds. This life is a life of renouncement.

Why should man live this life? Why should he die to himself? And why should modern man in the times of worldly prospects, progress and welfare think of dying to himself or renouncing himself?

First of all: according to Martin Heidegger (1967, 55) man is a being for death. This is the basic dimension of man. Man has to give up in order to get anything in his life. A child will be conceived and born through the parent's giving of each other. All important and worthy things have their price. From this point of view, man is a being for death. Man should be ready to accept life as an open but limited (by death) process, as a motion and readiness to give up his own power to govern life and to accept the possibilities of otherness.

This involves accepting oneself and the other as limited and in the same sense readiness to empathize with the other, which means to die to oneself. This brings possibilities for dialogue between partners. Edith Stein stressed the importance of empathy for the survival of mankind. She accepted her fate as a sacrifice for her nation and a sacrifice for the salvation of the German nation. But is this empathy possible without such faith as Edith Stein had? Only free existence prepared to be given to the other (Levinas) can be emphatic.

The outer world cannot give man such primary experience. A child will learn the empathy only through inner meetings with other person (Erzar/Kompan). A child will be open to experiences of empathy by the parents. If (s)he is learning to express his/her feelings, (s)he will give himself up to the other, learn to live in love, as well as meet God. Such childhood is the purpose – to change the habits of modern consumptive life and to come to the sources of life. This will be reached by dialogue.

Dialogue as acknowledgement of the other and a way to the sources

The Christian culture is a culture of dialogue. The Old Testament speaks about the dialogue between Yahwe and his people. Partners tried to establish just relations. In the New Testament Jesus was practising dialogue even though he did not use the word "dialogue". The first Christian councils spoke about the dialogue in God as the Trinity. The relations in God are dialogical. This was the model for man, who is made according to God's image. In Western culture dialogue is the result of its long practice in Christianity, despite the fact that Christian communities did not always accept dialogical manners and also quarrelled and waged wars. Yet dialogue remained a means of overcoming conflicts between them. The Second Vatican Council also officially proclaimed dialogue as a form of meeting between different religions.

Dialogue is today regarded as a basic means for solving the world's conflicts, since we can choose between dialogising and destroying our civilisation. To follow the way of dialogue means to have sufficient ground for dialogue. Could it be only the fear of clashes between civilisations? Could it be the fear of wars or other violent conflicts? Dialogue opens a deeper insight into the mystery of man. Through dialogue among men and dialogue with God we find our mystical sources, which enable and persuade us to change our short-sighted and one-sided view of the world.

Dialogue and mystics

Many thinkers stressed that the 21st century will be either mystical or it will not exist at all. "Mystical" means the same as religious. Karl Rahner spoke about mystical in the sense that man should be open to the inexpressible. The real dialogue is expressed by poetic, mystic words, words that transcend usual daily experience.

Karl Jaspers speaks about "the ciphers of the transcendence." They are expressed through religion, philosophy and art. They are called ciphers because they express the last experience of man. This experience touches the limits of man's worldly experience and opens him to the inexpressible. Alois Haas distinguishes between the Buddhist and the Christian mystical experience. The Buddhist experience is nirvana, which means passing into the eternal "time and space", it is "void". The Christian experience of the self is a dialogue about Christians striving for the Otherness. It is the transcendence for the other world to come and openness to the Unknown. It is *via negationis* (Rahner 1961, 56). We have not heard the last word but we research reality in openness to the other (Other). Dialogue needs a new language and strives for the union with God. "The meaning of man's mystic union with God is all-extensive and total and have to do with totality of man's capacity." (Hass 2007, 25) There are different mystics and thus different paths to this unity, but it is important that these paths will be reached through finding new words (Theresa of Avilla). According to Master Eckhart, the word has tremendous power, "with the word could be wonders done." (Haas 2007, 107) Man plays a very important role in all processes of the world, he is a mediator of the world. This mediator's role can be performed in dialogue "among all opposites of the world." (Haas 2007, 268)

What can be the meaning of all this mystic inclusion in relation to dialogue? My aim is to stress that life has shadowy sides which should be opened in dialogue – this means integration, openness to all aspects of life. If we are ready to dialogize, we are taking into account the limited situation of our life in order to open ourselves earnestly in all our public and personal relations to new and deeper interconnectedness of our lives. It is a child who is open and accepts all things in life, willing to be influenced from different directions. We cannot take the world as the innocent, but in order to cope within and to deal with the world as such, we have to acquire childrenhood of God. Life as a technical project remains limited. The full life of man could be attained only by dialogue with all opposites of man's life and by preserving equidistance. Dialogue between two people and between man and God is the foundation of our lives which ensures our happiness.

Happiness

"And is happiness simply a matter of now anyway? Perhaps, as Aristotle sometimes suggests, happiness is better understood as an attribute, not of a present moment of one's life, but of whole life – the wisdom in the ancient Greek saying that we should call no man happy until he is dead."(Murphy 2009, 66) The Eckhartian, or be it the Christian attitude, is that the happiness is a paradox. Man will be happy if he is opening his life in dialogue to the otherness, yet it implies giving up his life. What it really means could be dialogised and could not be exhausted during our earthly existence, though we have no other access to it. So:

I am going to travel inwards

I am travelling into me

Into the inner core of my being

Where you are dwelling

At this deepest point of my being
You are still there before me
You are creating and reviving
Strengthening without ceasing
my whole person.

Dag Hammarskjöld (1905-1961)

6. THE CORPOREAL DESIRE AS A PROBLEM OF REALISING DIALOGUE

Body dilemmas and the materiality

In her book *Plato and Levinas,* Tanja Staehler (2010, 54) exposes the importance of human body for all human relations. Plato, Levinas and other thinkers (like Husserl and Merleau-Ponty) agree that the body is an important dimension of interiority of man, "which is involved in enjoyment and suffering".

First of all, the human body is different from other things, because our body opens us up towards the world. Plato stressed that the body couldn't be discarded – against the common meaning that Plato treated the body within disdain, stressing only the spiritual dimension of man. According to Levinas (and Plato) the body "opens us up to the world as well as to *logos*." Furthermore, the body is an organ, which makes the "exchange and even reversibility between me and the world" possible. This is very important for "any subject-object relation." "Thirdly, Levinas moves on from previous accounts of corporeality to stress that sensibility is intimately connected to vulnerability, thus adding an ethical dimension." (Staehler 2010, 55)

To sum up: according to Staehler, at Plato and Levinas the three aspects of corporeity could be seen: First, the body is different from other material things, because the body couldn't be separated from the soul. The body opens us up to the world and to the *logos,* too; it is a living materiality. Secondly, as for the body, there is a permanent exchange between us and the world (subject-object relation). Thirdly, according to Levinas the sensibility as a corporeal characteristic means vulnerability, too. This dimension causes troubles in relations between people and their relation to the material world. The body opens us to the world; it makes us receptive for other beings. The body is passive (receptive) to all other (things and beings), and is under their influence. They put an effect on it, and consequently, they leave their impressions on it. The man as a corporeal being is constantly under influences, which make the man receptive for all the streams of the environment. In this sense, the man is relatively speaking a product of the environment - as the societal theorists say. But there is not just the passive influence; it is a continuous exchange between a person and his/her milieu.

Because of this interconnectedness there are always troubles between the people, which concern the limitedness of the corporeal things and the unlimited desire of man after these things. The decisive point is among the men, concerning their relation to things they could have. It is not the problem between men and things but among the men and their desire for things they want to posses. The desire for things is a source of permanent quarrels among the humans.

There are no a priori rules, how one can access to other with respect to the things and this openness is the constant source of attacks, subjugations of self or other. Because of the relational complications rooted by corporeal structure of human beings, the community has difficulty to arrange these processes, to develop the rules or the symbolic forms, prohibitions and laws, to avoid the violence coming out of this relations and processes. This is the cause of regulation by rites and ceremonies to protect the community from violence. According to René Girard (1979) the humanisation of these complex tensions among individuals and communities is mythical or religiously founded. The most critical points to deal with this relation between the body and the soul are: the beginning of man's life - the birth, and the end of man's life - the death. In all cultures, there were rites to prevent (especially the young) people from the outburst of desired tensions at these lemits of life. They occur because of the corporeal dimension are constantly present in all deeds and processes of human life and cause struggles in the battle of survival, which are the sources of violent tensions among individuals and groups.

The power of sexual desire

The corporeal side of humans enables the man to be a sensitive being, because he can perceive the other human and all other beings. The corporeity is a concrete actualisation of the man which makes a human being finite/final, worldly and threatened being. The beginning and the first years of person's life are the most sensitive and dangerous because different influences are being balanced on her/him, but she/he is not enabled enough to rule them. They go through the body and leave the consequences on it. The openness and vulnerability of the corporeal being in this period of human life requires a maximum of engagement of all human beings to overcome respectively to solve these tensions. The sexuality plays the decisive role in bringing forward man's desire. The strongest rules and prohibitions were taken on the area of sexuality. Today, through different possibilities of media the sexual desire has become an unlimited possibility for violent exploitation, especially of the vulnerable and weak.

Because of this vulnerability of man as corporeal being and difficulties for different tensions to be put in order, the humankind has always been taking care to protect the young beings and to prevent obstacles and to secure the best development of individual and social life, especially in the first years of her/his life. The sexual desire determines the person very strongly, the relations among men and women and societal life of humans as whole, as the several scientists, especially psychoanalysts point out. The conception and birth touches mostly the grounds of man. It is a challenge for everybody to participate in the creation of the new human beings and to prolong his/her corporeal presence in this world. From the ancient times we can read about the hope of parents to have a descendents and to provide through them to live in them for next generations (Gen 22, 17ff.). The sexual act should be as a primer act of love. There are several obstacles that this occurs very seldom, because the sexuality of man is interwoven in so many different cultural, socio-economic, ritual and sacred contexts showing the complexity of it.

To perform this task the humans are provided by the sexual ability as the important power of man's life. The power of (sexual) desire expresses correctly the Plato's dictum that the desirable part of soul of everybody is mostly extended and insatiable (Plato 2013, 442a). The sexual as well as other desires are connected and interwoven into the causes of irregularities of human life. They all tend to incorporate the human life and also to make possible that man can express him/herself as a corporeal being as well as a being with feelings and emotions. "Sexuality leads to quarrels, jealous rages, mortal combats." (Girard 1979, 35)

As a desirable person the humans seek a completion of their endeavours in corporeal relations. Despite of all regulations of this life it is difficult as well for one as for the whole community to regulate these processes in the way to come to order in the society. The desires are usually not unlimited as Marcel Proust worked out in his first works. After his conversion in mind (Girard 2008, 270ff.), Proust understood that the real solution of this problem was the limitation of the desire: "Before his great change, Proust was a talented amateur. His conversion turned him into genius." (Girard 2008, 271) This conversion was in the right sight of the role of desire in man's life. The rules, rites and other cultural and religious regulations throughout the history take care especially for this part of our lives. As the most problematic part of human desire is the sexuality, man can usually transgress the rules and violently urge the woman. In all societal revolutions and wars men from the conquered side have raped women. How to attain conversion (Girard) about this main point of human life, is one of the most crucial question of humans.

Is woman a victim?

Why such violent actions against the powerless women? Is it just a natural sex's abreaction? Is it a 'natural' repayment action? Is it a psychological revenge for the bad childhood or bad social conditions of men, engaged in the wars? Is it only a possible reaction on the women's superiority over the men? Are there some psychological archetypes hidden behind this relational struggle? How to protect the humans from these deviations and to secure the survival of humankind? As Girard sees it, the prohibitions are made to protect the society from new outburst of violence: "Wherever violence occurs, a prohibition is proclaimed." (Girard 1979, 219) And he continues: "The victim will serve as a mediator, between the inside and the outside."(Girard 1987, 69)

Girard specially points out the violent danger of sexuality:"All this regulations serve to endow both sexuality and violence with the same centrifugal force. In many instances the sacrificial deviations of sexuality and violence are virtually indistinguishable. Marriage vows can be duly attended by ritualized violence resembles the endless cycle of revenge that might well rage inside if there were no substitute for it outside the community, and the reciprocal exchange of violence with outsiders is one with the exchange of women that provides men with sexual objects from outside the community…Beneficial and life-giving, but also dangerous, regulated sexual violence (like ritual murder) is surrounded by a veritable buffer zone." (Girard 1979, 220)

As for the violence, according to Girard, there are differences among the men and the individuals in the community and between the different communities, but there are no big differences between the hostile and economic aims: "Whether warriors are killed alternatively by one side or other, prisoners are captured, or women are 'exchanged', there can be little difference between institutions that establish agreement for the sake of hostility (assuring, for example, that neither of two sides will be deprived of ritual enemies) and institutions that promote hostility for the sake of agreement, providing for the exchange of women or goods that cannot be kept within the group. The 'cathartic' function dominates in the first whereas the economic function dominates in the second, but the two functions are not truly distinct. It is only by means of *a posteriori* rationalisation that we manage to obscure the common origin of all institutions, which is the reproduction of generative violence."(Girard 1987, 79)

Thus it is most important to provide the regulation of the violent excesses of (sexual) desire. The 'mimetic crisis' could be overcome through strong regulation in the communities; the innocent victims are needed to provide secure salvation of crisis. There are very welcome 'solutions' from outside. This 'regulation' from the outside usually happens in the wartimes. The soldiers use to rape the women and to take territories and food of the neighbour enemies. Thus, the wartimes, times of revolutions and of other societal riots are the extreme times of mimetic crisis and in this sense the extreme times of searching for the scapegoats. The societies have found out the mechanism to provide the "class enemies" and other "causes" for the solutions of mimetic crisis. The decisive question is the interpretation of the real status.

The strongest, most influential desire, the sexual one, plays the leading role in these processes. The mimetic crisis in this area tends to be overcome through the total overpower of the rivals, raping their women and through conception preserving the power over the rivals after their death, too. The modern women miss the human nearness and warmth, they are unsatisfied and they rebel against the men. Then the unsatisfied men revenge against the women to fulfil their lack of women's love in their previous (child's) life.

The first reason is the anthropological one. The wartime gives the men an opportunity to show their power over the women, although otherwise they are dominated by them (women). Secondly, the warriors could perpetuate (maintain) the dominance over the rivals through the raped women and conceived children, probably the future slaves. This performance should take place collectively and ritually if to become a sacred value – a sacred war. It must happen in sacred rite and in a public ceremony. The performance is perfect if the tormenter succeed to persuade the victims to collaborate and to confess their guilt: "The mimetic collaboration of victims with their executioners continues in Middle Ages and even into our time…In our own times all forms of Stalinism find viperous victims who will confess far more than is asked of them…" (Girard 1989, 64) The mere victims of the communists in the Slovenian post war time were trained to be bearers of the consequences of their relatives, who were killed by the same communists. Many of them took over the most dirty societal works and some of them still perform them today. The authoritarian society does not encourage mutiny against the terrorism. According to Bauman the totalitarianism is possible per obedience. Even the rulers of the slaves are interested in what their slaves are thinking. All totalitarianisms have a secret police to gather their opinions. All these were not only the cases going on during the war on the territory of former Yugoslavia but in other totalitarian societies, too. The victims are paralyzed and persuaded as being guilty and are prepared for the "holy offering". There is a sacrificial blood which plays a decisive role in these sacrificial rites.

The ritual blood

The blood is a living sap, a substantial part of man's body and symbolizes the life as whole. The blood will be shed for the survival of man. It has an important or decisive role in man's life. Girard points out that the menstrual and the victim's blood opens the similitude of blood's sheering: "On the other hand, to understand the impurity of menstrual blood we must trace its relationship to blood split by violence, as well as to sexuality." (Girard 1979, 34) All these dangerous processes and completed realities of man need the regulations and have a ritual and sacred dimension. So religions and rites took essential part on performing this task. To prevent the intimate sphere of wo/man the society has to take care for the forms of behaviour in this area: "Sex and violence frequently come to grips in such direct forms as abduction, rape, defloration, and various sadistic practices, as well as in indirect actions of indefinite consequences. Sex is at the origin of various illnesses, real or imaginary; it culminates in the bloody labours of childbirth, which may entail the death of mother, child or both together." (Girard 1979, 35)

Mostly in these processes the victims are women like in the Canadian myth of Dogrib Indians, where "a woman has intercourse with a dog and gives birth of six puppies" or in "Jewish woman from Binzwangen accused of giving birth to pigs." Girard continues "because the scapegoat mechanism is at work throughout and becomes fundamental."(Girard 1989, 49/50) This confirms crucial and leading role of women in the society and its processes.

For women, the rape is not only a case of violence but at the same time treading down of their honesty. They lost their own homes and property; perhaps they gave a birth to a child and were expelled from their communities, away from their relatives (Yuval-Davis 2009, 170). It is a usual procedure in Islamic communities, although other societies practise it, too, as it is a question of the honesty of tribes especially family-clans or a nation, as it was the example in the former Yugoslav wars.

Furthermore, the mutilated girls testify about the leading role of women in several societies too. The mothers, grandmothers or other women play the decisive role in these rites of mutilation of young girls. The mutilation of sexual organ of girls is a violent ritualistic action over the innocent young women. Surprisingly it takes part in several autochthon tribes and also in several Islamic societies today and most surprisingly it occurs in western countries, too. The ritualistic executors are the women. The sexual blood is shed to preserve the traditional balance in the society.

To preserve the order in the society is a case too; a woman who has been sexually abused by man, or who has committed adultery, should be stoned. She becomes a double victim: a victim of sexual abuse as well as of stoning. It would be necessary to investigate why it is better to offer the innocent woman instead of the married man. Perhaps the marriage's institution should be preserved and therefore the woman should be offered. There are societies killing newborn girls to secure their survival. The women are forced to participate in such acts. In this way, there are girls or boys sold for prostitution, work or terrorist activity with the only reason for the clans to survive.

To preserve the order

There is an agreement among the communities to solve the mimetic crisis through definitive ordered acts, which are regulated by the traditions of rites, prohibitions and other religious-cultural orders. Their main intention is to find and to provide for victims who enable the sustaining of societal order. The arrangement of offering has a cultural background which is in general ordered in a way that the weak has to be a victim. The societies provide the ways of arrangement among different societies to perform this task and to choose a victim just to overcome this mimetic crisis. The decision to decide upon the victim finds several adequate ways and agreements through societal institutions and their different mechanisms. It is a question of cultural consciousness, a question of interpretation: "Human behaviour is determined not by what really happened but by the interpretation of what happened. The double transference guides such interpretation. It transforms the victim into something radically other than, and transcendent to, the community. The community belongs to the victim but the victim does not belong to the community." (Girard 1987, 78)

Nevertheless, there are still women in modern societies being the victims and at the same time taking the main and decisive role in such processes.

The sexual violence and the Christians (Catholics)

Girard says: "We are tempted to conclude that violence is impure because of its relation to sexuality." (Girard 1979, 34) This is a problem among the Christians too. Despite that Christian teaching stresses the real role of victim in the society, through ages; Christians took part in violation of human rights and in persecutions of the victims, bearing the exclusion from the community in common. It is the Christian understanding of sexuality that plays the decisive role in such relation to the victims and processes against them. It was usually seen as a prohibited (sexual) action if not procreation's act, but not so much by means of human relations. The human dimension of sexuality and especially the sexuality of women was put aside. In this sense the sexuality has still been the taboo, and therefore not included in the normal human relations. The Christians are told to oppress it. This suggests the art of celibacy's obligations for the men who are to become catholic priests. The stoic's heritage played an important role in these processes.

There are several victims of these processes. One of them is the catholic priest as a victim of such oppressive system of the church. He is chosen from the people to perform the prayers and sacrifices, but he belongs no more to the community as he is taken out of it and has a special status of victim. He is no more a "normal man". Therefore, he is separated from the other and put to be sacrificed for others. He is not only a chosen bearer of the Christian freedom available for all people, but also a captive of the Church's system.

The other victims in the Church are women who have to submit their lives to man's desires. The biased interpretations of sexuality do not permit to see the sexuality as a personal process between a man and a woman.

Through ritualistic and lawful order the Catholic Church performs the strategies to retain the power over the faithful people and to make them victims. This religious life is not stimulated by Christian teaching of the non-violence and care for the weak man, but by the obedient order of the church.

On the other side, through advertising, the sexuality in today's society is made to serve to commercial process, which victimizes the ordinary people.

Modernity and violence

Through emphasized commerciality the desire is increasing. We have perceived the unlimited growth of desire of the "few". Their rivalry excludes the "many", who have possibility to see the goods, but they don't have the chance to get them. Therefore, the victims today are "many" whereas the "few" succeeded through financial and political power to keep control over the most capital in the world. The "few" don't have any instruments to prevent these processes of the "many" and to make anything against their bad status, the global violence is heaping: The corruption is the biggest threat of humankind. The president of The German *Transparency International* Edda Müller states that "without trusting the elites and institutions and without our personal experience that the man/woman can reach success and respect by behaving morally, our society will in a long term collapse." (Müller 2010) Hence, the main problem is the full respect of a human.

The respectful behaviour needs profounder sources. To make a decision for a non-violent behaviour towards others, the man needs faith and hope that every living being should be respected. This faith is grounded on the supposition of a deeper insight into the reality, which is usually understood as a religious act.

If there were religiously founded rules and rites to secure the societal order and to prevent the escalations of the violence in the past, this is no more the case of today. The individual is lost in the open global circumstances. It is expected that one will decide all by oneself. But there are new media and socio-political order which does not provide for the individual to react in such complex situation. Therefore, the individual becomes the victim of these processes. The post-modern man is more and more lost in the global world, a world without rites and rules of behaving. The totalitarian order sacrificed the behaviour of all, the (post communist) transition and global changes make uncertainty and societal disorder. The today's status is that of exclusion of many and the preference of the "few", which leads to escalation of societal tensions. The main victims are the millions of poor people, dying of starvation and several diseases. The reasons are the changes of the global society, which causes the downfall of the traditional societal order and do not provide for the new rules and frameworks to protect the individual. The process started with the beginning of a new social class of workers, who were put aside in the society and the old classes wouldn't really accept them as a part of the society. This causes disturbances and revolutions. It has been going on in different forms until today. Especially brutal have been these processes in Africa. The number of victims of such processes is increasing all over the world, especially after the fall of communistic systems.

The Catholic Church used to be and still is a scapegoat for all these troubles, mistakes and other irregularities of the modern society. It has been the ethical and spiritual engine of the modern society and concludes these processes (Vattimo 1997, 44-52). Several times the Churches and religious organisations took part on the oppression of the victims. The consequence is the tension to accuse and make the Christians and the Catholic Church as a scapegoat for these unsolved societal problems. Especially in the case of Church being a 'sacral' institution. By means of electronic world and new media it is easy to make the Christians and the Church as an institution a scapegoat for all the troubles, the killing etc. as they have been those who critically observe the state oppression, state regulations, like in regimes of communists and Nazis. The examples are Archbishop Romero from Salvador or priests and Christians in Amazonas, who work against cleansing of wood or the Catholics and other Christians in Islamic states like the executed Bishop from Turkey

Luigi Padovese (1947- June 3, 2010). The societal revenge especially in the post-communistic countries can be easily burdened in the Church and among the Christians. They have always been made for victims and therefore excluded from society although they belong to it. There is always a sacred ritual performed to bring a "finishing solution" (Hitler), to kill enemies of Islam etc. The rivals should be destroyed and thrown out of the society, too. The purpose of these "sacred" rites' performances is to control these processes of disorder in the post-modern society. The exclusion of the religious attitude from the societal sphere caused and still causes a silent consensus in the societies that the religions are necessary a source of violence. This was the case by the development of the society in Balkan especially in 20th century and it could be seen in other Marxist countries too. This is a crucial problem not only for the nations of this area but over the world. Because in the modern societies the talk about "religious violence" is prevalent, the question arises why this relation is so much stressed in the modernity, despite religion being already driven out of the modern individual and public consciousness. And it is very surprising that many authors that are interested in connecting the term religion with violence do not have many persuasive arguments to show that this claim is justified.

The Christian thinking of non-violence

There was Mahatma Gandhi (1987, 134 ff; 155ff.) who stressed again the importance of the Christian teaching of Blessings. Gandhi made a synthesis of Indian sources of non-violence and Gospel's Sermon on the Mount (Blessings) of New Testament (Mt 5). The Blessings are a forgotten chapter of Christian's tradition. In short, the Spirit of Christ is a spirit of pure heart, of truth and justice, of non-possession and non-violence. The Holy Spirit as a Paracletus is an advocate of man believing in Christ. He works if somebody is ready to convert (*metanoia*), which means not to go the ways of this world. Therefore, this *metanoia* is a personal act, not public (general) decision and does not have much popularity and maybe it is not influential. But it should be - as everybody is addressed to take part in this process. Perhaps many need a good example of the truly Christians or truly humans and there is a need for such education on several levels. This is namely a decisive question of our survival: If we are able to develop the (ethical) attitudes to provide the individuals and groups and also the whole society to work non-violently and to share the things empathically and dialogically, we can hope for the future of mankind.

If we want to get the changes in the environmental processes in this world, there is no alternative to this *metanoia*. These changes imply the changes in mind and the readiness for empathic dialogue with others. This is a religious process and could be reached without the religious reasons, as the change in mind is a religious act and because the Christian way and human way could be undertaken only religiously. We can believe that these religious or faith processes are truthful human processes and therefore ethical processes. In my opinion this could be – in addition or completion to ethics' projects of Küng (1990) or Dalai Lama (2004) – a sufficient reason for ethical changes in humans. There are no other chances to solve the problems of humans. There are enough reasons for humanity to be prepared for it and there are humans to be ready to undertake these processes and to help to change the direction of development of this world.

Peter Sloterdijk enumerates ten obstacles of the modernity to achieve the philosophical status (habit). The philosophical and theological status means to oppose the life: Paul Valery wrote: "The essence is against the life." (Sloterdijk 2010, 125) This *metanoia* is describing the philosophical habit in details. It is an *ars moriendi* as the Christians of Middle Ages said or as Fichte pointed out "the knower is the functioner of the Absolute" (114). He has to die himself to be a bearer of the spirit. According to Sloterdijk this is the so called spiritual training. The philosophical (and much more the theological) man has to be trained; it is an asceticism of a life in a continuous epoch in a continuous episteme, in a constant observation of the essence.

7. ARE VICTIMS REQUIRED FOR MANKIND'S SURVIVAL? - PROBLEM OF THE EXCLUDED

A being of leisure

Man is a being of leisure, not ready for profound changes in himself and in the society. One of his (negative) properties is to persevere in his old stage and miss opportunities to change his life for better. This is the case with individuals and the society, in our own life and in the lives of others. Many opportunities for good individual and social life are lost because of this, and much more should be offered to make such changes afterwards. The changes after the First World War did not offer opportunities for self-determination of nations. Despite tens of millions of victims, the end of the Second World War brought no freedom for all. Rolf Zimmermann analyzes in his book Moral as Power (2008) the moral side effects in the politics of the last centuries. He tests the morality of the politics in the genocide of Armenians, Jews, Chinese by Japanese, and different nations and groups by the communists. Why were these groups being murdered? Are the events like holocaust and other genocides of this historical period products of the nihilistic technical era, as Günther Anders stressed (Anders 1992, 1996; Zimmermann 2008, 92), or is this a product of the modernity with its technical equipments, which made possible such criminal enterprises, as Bauman (1994, 27) stressed (cf. Zimmermann 2008, 90). Against the non-differentiated thesis of Anders and Bauman, according to Rolf Zimmerman, the modernity could develop an adequate democratic structure to prevent such terrible events. This means that these deeds do not stem necessarily from the development of the modern world, but are caused by the lack of democratic culture. This means that man is not ready to adapt himself to the claims of human life's essence and to be open for a dialogue with others. Especially the European continental man is a man of a system, of authority and of the framework, in contrast the Anglo-Saxon is much more concrete from experience. In America this was caused by the necessity of the new-comers to cooperate that they could survive in the New World.

The continental framework's ways of thinking tend to exclude, and in the modernity it led to totalitarianisms. The dissonance between the political and spiritual sphere made the partnership between political and religious communities difficult, and brought about absolutist tendencies. There was the hierarchical-authoritative modus of the Church which supported the authoritative trainings of citizens. A Jewish woman who survived holocaust is convinced that the holocaust would not have been possible in England. On the other hand, the English were involved in many victimisations of the modern World. The lack of independence, autonomy, the will to implement dialogue, cooperation, and to include the weakest in the society everywhere led to non-living and authoritarian societies. Political power overruled or removed moral aspects of life. Nationalisms and class mentality demanded clean and closed nations in a single state, and caused also totalitarian exclusions. The fascination over capital and its exclusive rule over people did not respect the struggle for survival of the new societal class of workers and the peasants, which were being ruined.

This development introduced particular morals, like the class morality of communism, the national morality of the Young Turkish Movement, the racial morality of Nazism and Fascism, the Japanese ethnocentrism. Their problems are non-acceptance of moral universalism and the exclusion of some living parts of the (whole moral) human community; every categorical morality should include all people. According to the Charter of Human Rights (1948), all people should be granted basic human rights. Every morality which excludes any person or group is according to this Charter amoral.

The changes in 1989 also did not give satisfaction to the victims and their relatives. The new democracies are burdened by residues of past totalitarian exclusions; there are still only a few accepted democratic procedures in the society.

The same holds true for individual lives. Man is already burdened by his parents and other members of the society who are not ready to develop in him human potential, allowing others to take part in their own life. Lack of work on oneself and burdening others with one's own problems on the other hand brings about attacks on others, who thus become victims of someone else's unsolved problems.

Because the ethics is a practical science - art, the problems of the man and the society could be solved only by practical work. The ethical attempt should work in the human context which means that the ethical conditions for the relations among man should be worked out. This is the claim for the "horizontal ethics" resp. the "humanisation of moral"

(Pieper 2000, 135). From our perspective it means to exchange the humanity and to involve all people in the process of the humanisations. This is much more needed after all humiliation of humans from the totalitarianisms (Jaspers 1962, Jonas 1987) and all modern globalised procedures of world human communion. The humanisation means to take part in the problems of humans. Everybody should be involved in the procedures of searching the ways to take up the burdens of all humans. All humans should be taken as integer human and not just as a means for different purposes.

The new morality

Adhering to bad habits, taking easiest ways, and fixating on austerities impede the development of man's central and vital abilities, thus the development of the society. The consequences are the social crisis of the today's world. The real causes of the financial crisis, the Fukushima disaster and climate changes are moral ones. Safranski quoted Nietzsche, who said that "man is not ready to know radically and 'coolly', and he (Nietzsche) criticised in this sense as early as Socrates (and Plato)." (Safranski 2010, 121) The finding of truth (true knowledge) presupposes the ability to discern between good and bad, to be moral and to develop the "sense of humility". We need "more spiritual people": "The love of truth has a salary in heaven and already on earth." (Nietzsche 1988, 53; III/45) To make changes implies searching after truth of oneself and one's societal companions, and to acknowledge one's humility and anthropological limitedness.

The Nietzschean philosophy struggles for this moral self-picture of man. He saw the solution in criticising the Christian (and modern man of technics) view of man. The humbled modest Christian man should be replaced by a strong, more high and self-resolute man: the Superman. Because the Christian God has died, a new strong and powerful man should be born. The Christian morality should be replaced by the morality of this Superman – Zarathustra. He is an ideal man, a personification of morality and an incorporation of the new morality, the morality of power.

According to Zimmermann (2008, 156ff.), Nietzsche influenced most of the modern political movements: Mussolini's Fascism, Hitler's Nazism, and also the Russian bolshevism (Lew Nikolayevich Trocky) and

Zionism. Behind most of these influences is the Nietzschean idea of the self-redemption, which is a pillar of his philosophy. This philosophy advocates a modern, powerful, strong and exclusivist man. All these movements were built on Nietzsche's social philosophy, which promoted and cultivated special kinds of people: a concrete type of racial, national and class people. But it is impossible to accept all this Nietzsche's views of morality, like his badly grounded critic of the Christian morality and his exclusive view of man, which prefers special kinds of people and discriminates the others. We can understand his struggle for a moral man and accept his endeavour for high standards of morals, but we cannot accept his views that some kinds or types of men are moral and other not, because this means to exclude some people from the human (moral) community. And this was the case with Fascist, Nazi and communist morality. These systems adopted Nietzsche for their instrumentalistic and imperialistic totalitarian purposes.

Nietzsche's and any other morality of this kind are to be criticized due to its exclusiveness and limitedness to a concrete group of people. In contrast to this, the true moral principles are applicable to everybody and have thus universal character and value. The morality should be applicable to everybody, it should be universalised, which means should protect everybody and prevent her/him for any discriminations. After post-Nietzschean era of the powerful man we have to find out what the true picture of man is.

Truth of man and victimisation

Because man is a being of reason, as the Greeks said, the problem of his knowledge is the touchstone. According to the Old Testament man cognitive ambition is to "be like God." (Gen 3, 5) Because man is not God and his knowledge is limited, the limitedness of knowledge is a supposition for truth of man. It is not in the first place a logical question but a moral one, the question of acknowledging his moral responsibility to others. The unwillingness to acknowledge this fundamental openness for truth of human reality is the cause and impediment to the knowledge of authenticity of human beings and thus the real humanity (Sloterdijk 2010, 135ff.). According to Sloterdijk, the Greek term epistéme testifies this openness for truths and confirms man's dialogical openness to the other and to the higher Good, God. But the modern economic and technological processes point out an "ideal man", man without deficits. Despite this, the modern man experiences imperfectness and disorders in him and in the society. This increases anger, dissatisfaction and unsolved tensions in individuals and in the whole society, and brings about a search for scapegoats, for the weak, who should help resolve 'the mimetic crisis'.

The scientific and technical acquisitions in the modern society not only culminated these tensions, but also introduced new standards of the man "of austerities". Besides this, the industrial development caused great disproportions in the society. Workers were the bearers of the 'modern development', but they get the least of its benefits. Peasants lost their base for survival. And this story has not been finished yet. We are still struggling for solutions, and several groups of people are still excluded from societal processes. All those people are potential victims, and they became real victims of the societal changes in the last centuries. The problem has nowadays global dimensions. The indolence of leaders and institutions of the society (governments, aristocracy, the new class of capitalists, churches) causes revolt of upper classes, peasants and workers, whose position is becoming more and more unbearable. Oedipus as a victim has become worldly – with global dimensions. According to Adienne Lezzi-Hafter (2000, 1131/2), "Oedipus is very important in modern literature and philosophy. 'Oedipus has any Oedipus' complex, but Oedipus is an Oedipus complex." Man remains a complex being, his challenge is a passion and permanent victimization. This complexity made many people strangers to the society: from modern slaves at the beginning of modern times to workers, women and children as excluded classes of the society. Today this processes culminated in the status of global workers. These are victims of luxuries of the modern consumer society: organised trade of modern slaves: women and children for prostitution, war and drugs (Cacho 2011). The modern Oedipus is entangled in the wealth of modern productive procedure, which produces masses of victims.

All these processes are against man. According to Paul Valery, "the essential is against life" (Valery 1993, 629; and Sloterdijk 2010, 125), or we can say the modern life is against the essence of man. The main processes go on without man's personal decisions and do not serve the true prosperity of man or the prosperity of most people. Man is a prisoner of these processes, and there are more and more victims in general:

modern consumers, the majority of poor global masses, but especially starving people, children and (young) women exploited for prostitution, cheep work, wars and drugs.

The Greek and the Christian view of man exposes the meaning of a victim for the survival of the humanity. Most of the non-Christian cultures prepared systems of victimization to prevent order and stabilization in the society. According to René Girard's late work *I see Satan fallen from the sky*, people knew that victims are necessary and systematically designed frameworks to justify their survival. Despite this, we have today extensive (verbal) care for victims, yet we cannot be proud of such care. After the end and fall of totalitarian regimes appeared new methods to victimize several groups and nations. Their number is still increasing. We are witnessing masses of victims, and there are many mechanisms (politics, media) to conceal this. We can paraphrase Girard by saying that the old myths were replaced by new (modern) ones (Girard 2006, 183ff.). Rivalries take place and the victims of this crisis of the humanity are increasingly excluded. The consequence of this development is the exclusion of most people from the goods of this earth. Let us look at it from economic point of view (besides other points of view), in numbers: there are 10 million millionaires who possess over 39 billion dollars. In contrast with this, 2.6 milliard people have to share only 1.4 billion dollars (Immel/Tränkle 2011, 56). The human searching for truth has to take care for this very important dimension of the truth of man today and find the solutions how to distribute the goods we have on this Earth.

The imperfect man searching for truth

Man of modern times was understood as a settled and scientific man, who stimulated, guided and governed the world and himself by science and technique. He perceived himself as a big, strong man empowered by science and technique. These are the prolonged organs of man (Kiepas 2010, 13). Man has a powerful sense of himself, which stimulated the faith that he would master the whole world. Nietzsche struggled against this monstrous man by inventing the individual superman, full of life and power. But the historical and societal limitedness did not and does not allow all people to get or to gain this ideal picture of man. Hannah Arendt (2005, Fall Dawn of National State and the End of the Human Rights,

345ff.) in her work *The origins of totalitarianism* analyzed the history of the totalitarianisms of the 20th century as an usurpation of human rights. Only men who were true according to these totalitarianisms were granted perfection in contrast to others, who were excluded, diabolised and considered bad. The ideas of racism, nationalism, chosen classes and the "better people" prevailed. (They were usual for ordinary people, who had to serve the 'best classes' and refer to them as 'better people'). A contribution of the mimetic theory of Girard stresses the "anthropological constancy" (Uhl 2010, 323) of the rivalry, which makes the "other", the weak, who are to be victimized, declared bad and guilty for bad conditions of man.

René Girard resumed the basic Judaeo-Christian topic of man: every man is a limited being, there is an "original sin", due to which there are not only bad or good, all are involved in victimisation and guilty. It is not possible to exclude and not to see the breaches of human existence. Man is an individual being, a divided being and thus imperfect being. To obtain this consciousness means to convert (*metanoia*) and be related to the other as a completeness of oneself. It means to be open for real relations to the other. Without this fundamental change, work on oneself, individual and societal reconciliation are not possible. Anybody could undertake to change his relations to others, but nobody can do it without acceptance of the other. Change begins in mind. If man is not ready to change his mind, he will persist in the habits and customs he already has.

Nietzsche also understood this hour of truth of man and wrote about extrapolation of modern man and tried the ways to change it. Like many modern thinkers he saw the problem in the Christian teaching of a humble man. He was aware that this is not also a man of technique, but a self-confident, powerful man inspired by the Greek *agon* (strife). The liberal paradigm of modernity strengthened this agonal, struggling and excluding relations among people. The Christian endeavour for interpersonal relations was thus reversed to rivalry and exclusion. Perhaps Nietzsche was beside of his psychological problems influenced by those modern tendencies and he saw the solution in a strong, powerful man who could change the modern strong systems which overruled the man. But according to Zimmermann (2008, 159), the Nietzschean ideal of man could and should be universalized in sense that all people are invited to realise the moral ideal of man. But this is not a man of technique, science, political (totalitarian) or consumer system, but only a "human

man". Because of it the solution could be very difficult reached in this world. There is no "hyper-policy" (Zimmermann 2008, 157), the instrument of regulating this is no totalitarian system, no classless society, no world policy.

Such a man should implement universal moral power (Zimmermann 2008, 159). This calls for universal rules or ways of dialogue. The ways of reparation of humanity are the ways of dialogical man, of enlargement and deepening of his morality. Human dialogue is a struggle for acknowledging imperfections of everybody and implementation of inter-human relations. Nobody should be excluded from these processes (Dumouchel/Dupuy1999, 170/232). The insatiable rivalry and unlimited enlargement of envy lead to more and more exclusions and do not allow the processes of reconciliation in the society. Dialogue among men should for this reason be completed by dialogue with God. Julia Annas (1994, 238) says: "The consciousness of the existence of ideas comes more from the conversion of the heart as from enlargement of intellectual sharpness." Paul Ricoeur thus terms the search for truth faithfulness. He speaks about "faithfulness of memories, of memories being true to …, in order to express this search, this demand, this claim, which constitutes the veridical-epistemic dimension of the *orthos logos* of memory." (Ricoeur 2004, 55) Peter Sloterdijk (2010, 132-147) demands the "objective respectively epistemic view", which means holistic, (enough) deep view or the belief, which is directed to truth. One should be peritus skilled (Greek: *epistéme* means skilled, scientific, firmly). He warns that the humanity of today, together with intellectuals, is more concerned about killing truth than about discovering (finding) it.

This means that the *metánoia*, the conversion to full dialogue, which frees man from his entanglement in the myths of mimetic desire, averts him from victimisation of others and makes him ready to participate in processes of memory, which certificate his belief and faithfulness. Ocvirk[2] is convinced that the *metanoia* as a Christian universalistic term is not applicable in the present secular society, which thinks in racial categories. The conversion to dialogue and to partnership can take place only (using Plato's diction) by memory of the eidetic world. So the supposition of Zimmerman to respect the Charter of Human Rights or to practice the universal morality is possible only by supposition of *orthos*

---

2 Cf. Ocvirk 2011

logos. This is the way to reconciliation and suspense of victimization. It is possible, because man has predispositions to good, but this should be always cultivated by dialogue (Ricoeur 2004, 491) and the will for truth. Ricoeur mentions that in the "ultimate act of trust there is no recourse but to assume an ultimate paradox proposed by the Religions of Book" and which Ricoeur (2004, 490) finds "inscribed in the Abrahamic memory". This dialogue is very difficult in the global society and in the Slovenian post-communist circumstances. The world crisis is caused by unwillingness to engage in dialogue, the Slovenian society is still permeated with the old Marxist manners.

Therefore, there are many sophisticated exclusions taking place in the modern world. Many people are made for victims, and are excluded from all societal processes. The violence has taken new and differentiating, subtle ways (trade with humans, terrorism, 'religious wars') which are consequences of these separation's processes of modern world. There are no possible ways for many people to avoid such circumstances of modern world.

Slovenian case

The Slovenian revolutionary case was a touchstone for creating a strong, revolutionary modern man without any compromises. This caused the fratricidal war which marked the Slovenian nation, and whose consequences are still felt. After the changes in 1989, we are still in the revolutionary euphoria, which takes mimetic dimensions at several decisive times, like in election campaigns etc. The dialogue among the divided parts has not taken place yet, because the post-communists believe that exclusions and rivalry is politically profitable. There are still many people affected by fear of the oppression from the former regime. The post-communists fear that the atrocious deeds of communist oppressors will be brought to light. The revolutionary values still prevail in the society. The mental, administrative and economic revolutionary revenge still takes place and hinders the reconciliation in the society.

The class enemy is predominant societal formula for exclusion of others and for maintaining the division of the society. The victims of the revolution are nameless, without graves, without compensations for their suffering. In this sense the post-communists are not ready to accept the principles of democracy. There is an ambivalent role of the Christians and the Catholic Church. The Church was in opposition to the regime. The Christians were prosecuted, exiled, more than 20,000 were killed during the war and revolution, the majority of them in the aftermath of war. Many Catholics were subjected to oppression and persecution by the secret police, there has been no lustration processes, be it political or in the Church. Many members of the Catholic Church still repeat the slogan of prosecution of Catholics. In general: the mentality of fear, isolation, powerlessness and rivalry as a sediments of the past system prevail instead of the trends of world's societal, economical and political processes. Slovenia will seriously begin with the reconciliation processes when the victims of the revolution are decently buried and the national declaration of reconciliation will not be only signed but politically and administratively accepted and implemented. They had to be declared as victims, so that other people could survive.

There was the moment in 2009, the 3rd of March, when the victims at Huda jama near Celje were discovered. After the long and tiring search and the removal of 100 meters of barriers, the excavating group found 427 fairly preserved corpses. Yet the search was stopped despite the fact that there are still more than 2000 corpses in the cave. The media showed the pictures of victims which moved the nation, and the compassion and empathy prevailed for some days. Under political pressure this lasted just about a week, afterwards political pragmatism prevailed over humane sentiments.

The disarrayed state makes, besides the old victims of the past regime (convicts, wronged parties, socially excluded), some new victims, newly socially excluded: workers, young generations with nothing to look forward to.

People in Slovenia are involved in the some processes of exclusions and with the same reasons as people from modern world, comparable to the world's processes but the revolutionary case gives the processes a special accent. From one point, it is the pragmatic reason which dictates the new transitorily class of the post-communist to survive by the manner of exclusion like it was in the communistic system. From the other side, the agonizing, rival mechanisms of consumer society leave more and more people aside of the societal processes. Because of the manner of communistic rivalry doctrine many people could turn to the dialogical ways of communication.

Empathy, dialogue and reconciliation

Jeremy Rifkin pointed out that dialogue and empathy are on the increase in the global society. He is aware that it is "the climb to a Global Peak Empathy" (Rifkin 2009, 423), which means that it is a very difficult task. On the other hand he is convinced that it will be reached. There is no doubt that it is a necessary task to reach freedom, reconciliation among different, mostly quarrelling human groups. There is an enormous need for empathy, but the ways to it are very difficult, combined with metanoia, with the change from rivalry to cooperation, compassion, and thus to the real essence of man. The agon, the logic of competition and revolution, still prevails, and not only politicians but also intellectuals, like Slavoj Žižek, promote and support theoretically and practically the revolutionary logic (Žižek 2009).

Rifkin speaks of the "births of humanism" (Rifkin 2009, 270), but could it be promoted by mimetic rivalry and 'scapegoat mechanisms', "the ones of really satanic relations-frameworks among men." (Uhl 2010, 318) This competition's mechanism among men should be converted to cooperation, dialogue and "solidarity with a suffering human being". Because so many people are speaking language of oppression and exclusion, the conversion is much more needed, but also much more difficult. We need prudence and ethical binding and responsibility.

According to Rolf Zimmerman, there are some criteria for historical moral responsibility. Generally observed, human rights are the criterion for meeting of people. We should not accept any particular moral criteria, the Kantian general law is to be observed. It is a frame worked out in the Charter of Human Rights from December the 10th, 1948, and it was worked out in detail at the conference in Vienna in 1993. The universal value of the Rights should be obtained. The human language has to take care for the intersubjective exchange of moral responsibility. States have moral responsibility for this communication. They have to deal with application of human rights in the historical and political area. The moral criteria of human rights should be globalized. There could be some particular cultural differences, but these should not go in different cultural blocs or different political powerful ideologumena, they should be discussed at the universal human level to suspend ideological particularities (Zimmermann 2008, 160-170).

The human rights should be cultivated and protected for "lower people", who are all humiliated, too. They have to take in account that their humanity should not be given up. It is very important to make the pedagogical and media campaign to persuade all people to take such care for themselves. Political and other rulers have to open and to explicate frameworks of the genocide of Armenians, the holocaust of Jews, other nations and groups, and removal of “class enemies”. In Slovenia and everywhere else the process of reconciliation exists, a long and difficult process which presupposes a conversion of mind and readiness to cooperate. The logic of revolution, which means lying, oppressing and exclusion, should be replaced by search for truth, freedom, cooperation. The latter are anthropological values, but to implement them we need steady willingness for dialogue at all levels of the society and in individuals.

8. SUICIDE AND GENOCIDE IN THE CONTEXT OF MODERNITY

The article is divided in three parts. This first part is dealing with the societal conditions of modernity which were radically changed in the new ages by development of science and technics. The second part I am speaking about problems of suicide and genocide under these conditions. The third part deals on attempts to access these complex problems of the modernity.

Part I

Introduction

The society of modernity comes to the labyrinths, because of the person's will to regulate her life but her inability to ménage it. This is the cause of the disorder and sideways, which radical quaked the human grounds, commenced the self-confidence of person and in her capabilities opened the problems of human self-regulation. This is still the problem of man of today and raises the question of human balance in self and in the world, because of it the question of meaning of human life and survival of human kind is posed.

Eugen Biser (1995, 267) wrote: "In the context of today's world, *conditio humana* (condition of human life) appears ambiguous: as a burden and as encouraging. Encouraging because, out of this conditions go initiatives, which consolidate human being in setting free his inexplicated capabilities and to transcendent status of his actual being in the acts of persistent making better of himself. But on the other hand he is actually burdened with complex of directive powers, which are turning himself from his own personality. This inflicts above all the basic human hope".

Concerning first part of this quotation the human life today is open towards new possibilities and in connection with this also insured with new discoveries of medical, pension, modern systems and discoveries of current civilizations. People, living in developed societies, used to live on track, based on fixed conditions, provided by science and technics.

We take out various insurances, which should provide us care in sickness and oldness; we create outer living conditions, in which we are supposed to live as comfortable as we can. We enrich our world with acquisitions for medical assistance, internet, radio, television... Our common day seems to be logically, completely, well-built and arranged and our life should be with no deficiencies. In short, life of individual should be in arranged framework, and this framework completely defines the life of individuals and communities.

These new discoveries and benefits for our life did in history of the modern era brought also disorders and sideways that radically shook fundamentals of human being putting doubts in humans and their abilities and opened a problem of human self-organizing, which still affect humankind. Consequences are troubles of human balance toward himself and to outside world, which opens a question about purpose of human life and surviving of humankind.

What does it mean? Vasily Grossman, Russian Jewry pointed it out in the novel *Life and Fate* that the time of totalitarianisms made strong the feeling of fatalism like it was the case under "Hitlerism" and bolshevism. We read about basic change in human and about lack feeling of their own and special personality and character. And all these make possible that "the feeling of fatefulness was increasing." (Grossman 1995, 204) The hero of the book, Jewish physician Sofja Osipovna "was wondering by herself that just some days were necessary to come the reverse way from human to the dirty and unhappy nameless livestock, plundered freedom, meanwhile the way to the human was going millions of years."(206)

Exclusion of others

The violent educational and political oppression against religious views shaped individual and societal consciousness, establishing a militant atheistic ideology, building an atheistic society, excluding others as different. These all continue as a burden in post-communist and other post-totalitarian countries. The phenomenon of systematic and violent "atheisation" without free individual and societal ways for individuals and the whole society in (post)totalitarian times remains.

This new "ideology of success dominates" (Girard 1989, 157) and the remnants of rivalry and exclusion of class-enemies became a practice. Still Girard argued that Christianity contributed very much to the real picture of victimisation and victims, but many modern authors didn't want to realize this (Girard 2001, chap. XIII). "In the future, all violence will reveal what Christ's Passion revealed, the foolish genesis of blood-stained idols and false gods of religion, politics, and ideologies." (Girard 1989, 212) Nazism attempted to absolve Germany and then the whole of

Europe from caring for the victims (Girard 2001, chap. XIV); the same can be said of Marxism. The exclusion of religion via accusation and establishing of violence is a "*proprium*" of modern ideologies which reaches its full realization in the totalitarian systems. The consequence of this "bad conscience" was the burdening of religions with predictive "violence", to diminish one's own violence, to excuse him, to "kill" the religious tradition of brotherhood of all people and to change societies with violent revolutionary methods. It has fatal consequences in the Balkans and in the wars of former Yugoslavia.

Exclusion of religious-spiritual heritage

Today we are facing a new challenge, a new moment in modern civilization, which Jacques Monod (1990, 281) describes "as rejection of centuries old spiritual tradition where spirituality is a decisive source of knowledge". The separation of politics and other spheres of societal life from religion is a complex process. The enlightenment project needs to be completed by addressing an important anthropological dimension of each person – the spiritual one (Wallach 2011). The lack of a religious-spiritual dimension caused wars in post-communist and other countries of different transitions, because the people had no ethical grounds to challenge the otherness but only posed the borders to the other viewing the other as a (class) enemy. Enlightenment's ideologies especially in their violent communist forms opened struggles against religion, as Casanova (1994, 24) stated: "However, as the Newtonian Enlightenment crossed the Channel, it became patently radicalized and militantly antireligious. Science was transformed into a scientific and scientist worldview which claimed to have replaced religion in the same way a new scientific paradigm replaces an outmoded one".

Gianni Vattimo (1997) asserts that Christianity played an important role regarding the origins of modern socio-cultural heritage. But the Enlightenment's attempt was to establish an autonomous anthropological or societal concept of "just", "moral" (Kant 1956) or modern "neutral" civil religion, in which God is an "empty sign" (Bellah 1991). We can find signs of this distinction in the works of many thinkers. Beginning with Locke (1955, 17; cf. Cavanaugh 2009, 80), as Ezra Kopelowitz (2003, 86-87) mentions, and after Locke "the religious-secular binary is a new creation that accompanies the creation of the modern state." (ibid.) Kopelowitz adds that the "distinction between the 'religious' and the 'secular' occurs in societies in which the individual rather than (the) group is the primary component of social organization" (ibid.). Individual persons were the ground of the modern state and the religion was thus considered to be a personal matter, and not a state issue. However this development causes dualism between the societal and an individual sphere or a kind of schizophrenia of person. On the one side the individual has his "own" religion; on the other he belongs to the national, political and to the religious community. The Marxists and other totalitarianisms benefited from it to subordinate the person under the totalitarian order. In particular the Catholic and other Churches trained their believers in obedience to make them available for their task. Religion was considered as a "private matter" but at the same time politics was trying to find a common (a-theistic) ideological ground or to span religious elements in state affairs. Casanova (1994, 21) enumerates for this modern development four reasons: "the Protestant Reformation; the formation of modern states, the growth of modern capitalism, and early modern scientific revolution". The last one was used as a parade horse of Marxism. These all implied the new organisation of modern societies with individualisation and search for the new ideological, non-religious grounds on which the society will be founded. This was not always the path toward subsidiarity but rather toward ideologization or totalitarization in the totalitarian systems, which remains an anthropological problem of former Marxist societies, because the Marxist ideology seriously injured human nature.

In the very beginning of this development it was the question of the role of religion in (modern) society. At the same time the struggle between the religious sphere of man and mankind on the one hand and the civil, so called "a-theistic" sphere on the other culminated in societal battles in the Modern Era. This was evident particularly in 20th century as the totalitarian regimes took total possession over the societal sphere, including religion. These "conversions" were accompanied by big societal disturbances, struggles and wars, (Alexander 1987; Pipes 1995; Snyder 2012). A private, individual religious sphere as a basis of the modernity was usually violently 'integrated' by so-called "a-theistic ideologies" or worldviews.

In modernity the experiences of religion were marked by many ideological and political dimensions, which were fixed by liberal: freemason (Alexander 1987, 30), socialist or so called civil, humanistic, "neutral", or non-liturgical (Hobsbawm 1983; Cavanaugh 2009, 113) worldview of man. Modern understanding of religion contained more political than religious connotations. Religion was expanded in the socio-political and strategic circumstances of modern development as was the case with the religions in BIH: "The traditional religion is privatized, while the religion of politics occupies the public realm". (Cavanaugh 2009, 116)

The myth of religious violence

"For its many avid consumers in the West, the myth of religious violence serves on the domestic scene to marginalize discourses and practices labelled religious, especially those associated with Christian churches, particularly in Europe, with Muslim groups. The myth helps to reinforce adherence to a secular social order and the nation-state that guarantees it. … The myth of religious violence is also useful, therefore, for justifying secular violence against religious actors; their irrational violence must be met with rational violence. … The myth of religious violence should finally be seen for what it is: an important part of the folklore of Western societies. It does not identify any facts about the world, but rather authorizes certain arrangements of power in the modern West. It is a story of salvation from mortal peril by the creation of a secular national state." (225/6) Tony Judt's (Judt, Snyder 2012, 98ff.) analysis of European history is a good example of the missing role of intellectuals with critical relations to the political power. To conclude this part: the modern society is a transition society, changing for centuries valid norms and habitudes, in case of Marxist regimes also the inherent anthropological values. The space of human was opened, undefined and challenging the human individual and societal capabilities. The liberal society doesn't secure the conditions in which it lives (Böckenförde 1976). So these conditions are influential for both, suicide and genocide. We proceed with some observations on suicide and genocide, which exposes its psychological and societal conditions and shows that the problem is arisen with conditions of life in the modernity and how the modern society tried to prevent these problems. The observations are supposing the previous statements and are dealing with legal and socio-cultural conditions and solutions to prevent genocide and suicide.

Part II

Suicide

"Suicide is an act, with which someone intentionally causes his own death" (SSK IV, 377), or "he execute himself" (Milčinski 1986, 11). Concerning Milčinski, somatic part has a crucial role at suicide (17). In opposite to him, Durrkheim (1992) emphasizes basically societal reasons for suicide. Milčinski searches reasons for suicide also in physical and mental conditions of individual. Trstenjak says, that suicide "depends on inner dispositions, we could say personal structure" (Trstenjak 1988, 576), which is not just personal of family determined, but also question of civilizations (of West) or as Lev Šestov (2002, 113) wrote: "Our century is labelled as century of nihilism par excellence".

Suicide is a very complex individual and societal phenomenon, but the societal conditions are very influential for it, as Emil Durkheim (1992/1887) stressed. As sociologists he emphasizes the cultural or social role of suicide. Like Durkheim also Fritz Riemann (1998, 15) sets connections between different types of humans through genetically determinations and early development of human personality.

Suicides are more common among men, which confirm that women are "strongest" gender. Durkheim establishes, that suicide is more common among Protestants, less common among Catholics and much less common among Jews.

Durkheim (1992, 69-72) divers between three different types of suicide:

1. Egoistical suicide, which concerns personality, which is concerned only about himself and of his own ego. This psychological type is the same type as first type of Riemann's fear of losing himself and inability to connect with other.
2. Altruistic suicide concerns personality, which is completely turned out of himself, towards others, towards society. This shows second type of fear, which concerns preserving himself, because of extroverted personality, and this leads to giving yourself for others, instead of growing up and become independent. Such suicides are and were for example Japanese kamikaze and Islamic terrorists, who are ready to give their own lives for their community (Riemann 1998, 199).

3. Anomic type means without law, what is the case when in the society values are not more accepted in the same sense and societal changes go so far that it comes to valueless system, in which individual feels uncompleted and empty. This situation we find in the societies of modernity and it is also a reason for growing number of suicides. There is a very urgent problem of transition in several post-communist countries too.

Durkheim (1992, 31) is discovering two different antagonistic forces: "The first one results from community and wants to incorporate individual; the second one comes from individual and denies the first one." Durkheim can be completed with observation that despite the social status is formally regulated are problem the weak relationships between humans. This is the cause that suicide depends on difficulties of social relations of individuals, beside the psychological reasons and mental diseases. We may conclude that crucial for preventing of suicide is good community. Beside this the psychic and psychological grounds have an influence on it.

Genocide

The *Declaration UN on Human Rights* in Preamble and Art. 4, 5 and 30 speaks of violation of human rights:

"Whereas recognition of the inherent dignity and of the equal and inalienable rights of all members of the human family is the foundation of freedom, justice and peace in the world,

Whereas disregard and contempt for human rights have resulted in barbarous acts which have outraged the conscience of mankind, and the advent of a world in which human beings shall enjoy freedom of speech and belief and freedom from fear and want has been proclaimed as the highest aspiration of the common people,

Whereas it is essential, if man is not to be compelled to have recourse, as a last resort, to rebellion against tyranny and oppression, that human rights should be protected by the rule of law...," (Preamble)

Art. 4. No one shall be held in slavery or servitude; slavery and the slave trade shall be prohibited in all their forms.

Art. 5. No one shall be subjected to torture or to cruel, inhuman or degrading treatment or punishment

The convention on Genocide prepared in December 9th 1948 and proclaimed in January, 12th 1951 give a definition and enumerates following "types" of genocide:

In the present Convention, genocide means any of the following acts committed with intent to destroy, in whole or in part, a national, ethnical, racial or religious group, as such:

(a) Killing members of the group;

(b) Causing serious bodily or mental harm to members of the group;

(c) Deliberately inflicting on the group conditions of life calculated to bring about its physical destruction in whole or in part;

(d) Imposing measures intended to prevent births within the group;

(e) Forcibly transferring children of the group to another group. (*Convention*, nr. 2).

SSK (1,676) describes genocide as "intentionally destroying national, racial or religious groups"; it talks about genocidal plan, crimes of the genocide, racist genocide and about politics of genocide.

History of the 20th century is covered with blood of genocide, began with Armenians in the year 1915, Ukrainians in communist Soviet Union in years 1932/1933, Jews in Germans concentration camps, afterward killings of the opponents of communism in Yugoslavia and elsewhere, mass murder in 1994 of Tutsis in Ruanda, caused by Hutu's extremist, genocide over Muslims in BIH, especially in Srebrenica in July 1995. The problem remains, and considers the way of asserting principles, by which we could sanction such incidents of humanity and against humanity in view of the ones responsible are usually connected with authority and do not confess their involvement in crimes, for example in Slovenian communism. Neither Resolution 1481 of Parliamentary Assembly of the Council of Europe (PACE), published on 25. January 2006 on Condemnation communism, fascism and Nazism, nor Resolution of Parliamentary Assembly of the Council of Europe (PACE), published on 2. April 2009 on *European consciousness and totalitarianism* of Parliament of EU of April 2nd, 2009 were proven as our own (Slovenian). And that is why neither anniversary of Slovene's Partisan's battle in

Dražgoše against Germans, nor anniversary of mass killing in Huda jama (Death cave), for us are not (yet) anniversaries of memory of the victims, but sadly still opportunities for false, ordinary and especially not human worthy political confrontations. Similarly the August, 23rd as Memorable Day of the victims of all totalitarianisms, does not have national-states based ground.

Modernity, Relationships – Exclusionist Competitiveness

Suicide and genocide are signs of disease condition of humans or humankind respectively human society. Both designate difficult conditions of humankind of modernity. Both are consequences of impairment if fundament human essence, which implicate as not normal behaviour in personal life or life of the nation. Specific impairment can experience those nations, who already suffered from some totalitarian system, which is the most significant challenge of modern world.

Trstenjak differentiate three different types of nations and individuals. Introversive personalities, like Slovenes, are more offensive against ourselves (and more prone to suicides) in like other nations, for example Albanians and the nations of the South of Europe. Here we can found some connections and reasons for aggression of modern society and why modern society is more prone to genocide and aggression against others. Trstenjak says: "…according to intra and extraversion human being can be more aggressive to himself or others." (575) This shows, how influence of social condition on both, individuals and nations, can be the reason for suicide and genocide.

Similarly, Eugen Biser (1995, 287) talks about "collective hospitalization", which is created by circumstances of terror and subjection in totalitarians systems.

According to researches of Arendt, Bauman, Snyder and others, we may say, that modern society almost forces human into aggression, and that is why suicide, as Trstenjak says in the same place, is more a phenomenon of Western society and its modern achievements, and less eastern society, which is more or fully spiritual, but this is changing now. The main reason, for Trstenjak, for lower rate of suicides on East is in primal way of living and higher rate, which shows on the West, because of artificiality of life. But there could also be more root cause: on the West, there are no sincere relationships. That is also why Trstenjak claims, that we cannot solve problem of suicide with SOS (emergency call). Suicide rate increases in periods of crisis of individuals (puberty, climacteric) and society (unemployment).

Suicide and genocide lead to (dis)trust. “Hope is not conviction in something would turn out good, but certainty, that something has its meaning, no matter how it turns out eventually.” (Havel 2012, 11) That is why neither suicide nor genocide, in anthropological sense, are at the end. As prisoners in concentration camp claims (Pahor 2008), there was no or few place for suicide or just thinking about it, but even though there was no escape considering genocidal plan. The victims of CC were full of hope and believed that one day, they will regain their humanity. Trstenjak concludes: “Despair is the strongest and the most convincing proof, that human is hopeful being. By the time he loses this hope, his existence converse to its opposite, when he cannot live anymore. Desperation is psychological fundament and predecessor of the suicide: desperation is the only right reason, why someone commits suicide, no matter direct cause and circumstances in which suicide was committed. To lose hope means to lose the meaning of life and power to strengthen the life. Both are connected. When someone lose (or cannot find) the meaning of his life, he/she does not have any reason to live forward, he/she does not have a strength to live, and this is the state of despair.” (Trstenjak 1988, 100) People living on the West are more susceptible to suicide, because they are afraid of suffering, which is confirmed with research about euthanasia. The older are afraid, that they would accept it, out of fear of loneliness and suffering, the younger, that they would be free of the older, who are burden for them. Suicides are rare in countries with lower living standard.

Similarly the genocide is a phenomenon of the modern society, which eradicates out of traditional values. Suicide and genocide are based on impersonal, systematical and lead by operative criteria of leading civilization.

That is why Trstenjak (1988, 582) presume arranged/ordered circumstances in order to prevent suicides. First meaning is psychological stability. Second meaning is certain isolation of common day or to be capable of transcend the common things among us, which he explain as personal faith or transcendent posture. For both is needed an exercise for harmoniously posture, as national saying says: “Do work as you will live forever, but pray as you may die today.” (584)

According to Eugen Biser (1995, 301), we are facing today a question about modern “humanistic illusion”. Either a human can rise above his own problems in order to solve them, or it means creating human-angel way to bestiality. With other words: Either the humans (humankind) can redeem themselves or we need a Redeemer/Saviour. This is probably one of the most important and basic questions of modern a-theistic and a-gnostic civilization.

It is very obvious, that suicide and genocide are phenomenon based on modern era. Reconciliation means the invitation of the Old Testament (3 Mz 23) which encourages humans for cooperation, reconciliation and for creation of sincere, solidary and basic circumstances for human being and humankind. Without reconciliation, which would reconnect people in-between we are more and more apart from each other, what results in loneliness, and as a result of this depression and suicide as recognizable phenomenon of modern society.

“To celebrate a life simply means to live it with others.” (Rifkin 2009, 165) Cooperation is a source of power and strengthens lives of everybody, and it is not an exclusion, that is why genocide is consequence of exclusion of some nations, groups of people, which enrolled in completely competitive relations of modern society. Snyder (2012, 379-421) in his epochal work describes reasons that lead people to killing or mass murdering of nations and certain groups in first half of 20th Century in so called bloody countries, that refers to areas in Nazis’ and soviet tyranny. The fight for supremacy, authority and enforcement and unacceptable social mechanisms, obedience, fear, big and small revenge, envy and opportunism, and other deviations from normal humanity contributed to our atrocities genocide during this period. Everywhere, the planners in humans, created moral dilemmas, after which they should, if they have ever been able, to face and examine it for the good of the derivation of the main objectives' but these things should be so carried out regardless of the price of the victims and the only necessary condition for the achievement of (large) goals. Still named Vasily Grossman (1995) describes in details the dilemmas and their horror and dispassionate in promoting the objectives of the systems goals, in which a man was the object. For us these things, according to Bolshevism, Lambert Ehrlich described in details in his work *The Russian Bolshevism* (1936) and *Bolshevism in China* (1936b). Everything and everybody are involved in a complex system of procedures by planners for the "anthropological changes" toward class or racial society of the so called "new" man. We were already warned about these excessive exits of modern society, such as Fascism, Nazism and Communism by Emil Durkheim (Kerševan, in Durkheim 147).

Part III

Modern Myths

William Cavanaugh (2010) speaks of modern Myths, which announced the salvation of problems of humankind in modern Age. As said many of them were or unfortunately still are cause of mentioned suicidal and genocidal threats. The modern society is trying to solve these problems by establishing of the new political, social and cultural measurement which are in some sense a replacement for the earlier (mediaeval) structures of society. The problem is that most of them are one-sided and burdened by lack of spiritual or virtue's qualification of individuals for this task. The development of modernity is reached structural but has a lack of inner consistence which could be a good interpersonal relations, trust of the citizens in the system and readiness for the responsible acting in the public sphere. The last one is no possible without the good spiritual or ethical condition of citizens. A decisive responsible acting is needed by public responsible persons, which seems to be a lack of these modern systems. If it no would be so, we hadn't a financial and structural crisis, as we have it now. The problems are very complex and the question arises what to do. First of all we have to analyze these myths of modernity and then to see which visions are possible after we were doing it. "Modernity is unaccustomed to regarding political theory as mythological in character." (Cavanaugh 2010, 9) The ground lies in the dilemma mentioned by Rousseau: "Man was born free, but it is everywhere in bondage." (Rousseau 1954, 2; Cavanaugh 2010, 9) To avoid the problems the modern liberal state is trying to develop a state theory in which the individuals give their freedom to be preserved and coordinated by state authority to prevent the violent tensions among them. Cavanaugh is stressing that the wars and other sideways of modernity were caused by these struggle for a modern liberal state (15-20) and the accusation for infectivity of this modern state were foisted to the religious violence (20-30). The modern liberal state remained as an untouched myth that the state would be the saviour of societal troubles.

"Far from coming on the scene as peacekeeper, we have seen that the rise of the state was at the very root of the so-called 'religious' wars, directing with bloodied hands a new secular theatre of absolute power." (46) The state was no saviour but a cause of imperialistic struggles which culminated in the totalitarian systems of 20th century.

The "myth of civil society as a free space" is a now a more complicated one. According to Cavanaugh is supported by many religious societal thinkers like Michel Novak (53) and Jon Courtenay Murray (54-62) in a sense that the civil space will filled the empty space of virtue's and spiritual dimension but without to do it with a some inclusion of theological language in the public discourse. Cavanaugh rightly asserts that theological language could not be excluded if we want that the theology functions in the society. Against the liberal doctrine he is asserting too with the most of communitarians that the virtues could be named and implemented in practical political life if we want that they will function in public sphere (88).

The last one is the myth of globalization as Christianity. Cavanaugh pleads for "as spatial story" (116). In the sense of political theology it is going "towards Eucharistic counter-politics" (46). We cannot go in the details of his presentation but to summarize up: he gives grounds for an open, public theological discussion and for questioning of the spiritual grounds and the open theological language. Can theology bring new hope?

Toward new hope?

Skrimshire (2008, 1) notes: "At the end of his 2004 Peace Lecture in Manchester, Noam Chomsky was asked this question from the floor: Do you live in hope, or despair? And his response was perhaps the most controversial thing he had said that afternoon: "it doesn't matter, I mean whether you have hope or despair is kind of like a personal matter between you and your wife and children or something, maybe not even that, it just doesn't matter, you do exactly the same thing, whether you're optimistic or pessimistic, really doesn't matter, it's a subjective question."

He comments this Chomsky's observations that "to ignore hope on the theoretical level … is surly to jeopardize a potentially powerful understanding of its practice." We need to deal with hope to react on our complex individual and societal problems.

To do this, we must implement a theological/spiritual view of reality, which will influence the daily life and is designated as a "Theo-politics". In the sense of biblical *kairos* there is needed a "fundamental *temporal* reorientation" (196). This includes the imperative for dialogue of politics with the theology. Skrimshire is referring to Cavanaugh's (2010, 86) book *Theopolitical Imagination* in which he insists that the Church has to be open for the public sphere in the sense of opening new spaces of politics, economics, social practices etc. This makes possible a new societal practice, "is a sense of urgency in integrating religious concepts and categories for reconceiving political practices of hope." (Skrimshire 2008, 198). He is hoping of "re-enchantment of the world" and suggests that "we must explore the question of hope through a variety of political, philosophical and theological languages." (199) In this sense it is necessary to transcend the empirical boundaries and to open spiritual grounds of man. According to Cavanaugh it couldn't be a universalistic but an interpersonal project. This is "a spatial story" as he understands the Christian Eucharist. We need concrete projects of working or resisting the established stage, or to be able for a "physical resistance". In the words of Cavanaugh this is story which "seeks to unify rather than divide" (116): "I will argue that the *Catholica* enacted by Eucharist is not a place as such, but a story which performs certain spatial operations on places….Stories organize and link spaces in a narrative sequence. They not only move from one space to another, but more accurately construct spaces through the practices of characters who trace an itinerary through story." (116) This is not a global (universal) abstract space but concrete every-day space. To give hope means to deal with concrete human spaces to make possible to exchange the stories and to unify.

Or in the words of Skrimshire (201): For Foucault's chosen context, the Soviet Gulag read the terrorizing and parabolizing effects of fear within the war of terror: We must open the eyes …to what enables people there, on the spot, to resist the Gulag, what makes it intolerable for the […].What is it that sustains them, what makes them stand and fight? […] The leverage against the Gulag is not in our heads, but in their bodies, their energy, what they say, think, and do."

There are the concrete people working towards unjust conditions in the society. The concrete Eucharist, the living faith and the practical oppression is a way against the subjugating of wo/men. The imagination of future, the openness for it means to deal with concrete reactions of society to prevent the total closeness of all posibilites, which is the basis of genocide and suicide. With Skrimshire: "Albert Camus said that only important question in philosophy was that of suicide, or, more precisely, whether or not life was worth living. My own investigations make it clear that the most important question facing society today is that of *political* suicide, which might also be described as the abandonment of imagination of future. A competing fantasy of the future operates today as a dominant security paradigm. A politics of fear. Today we inhabit, in a state of acquiescence, a terrorized present. How then, have these observations been the backdoor for investigating practices of hope? Camus' reasoning proceeded from a kind of curiosity for how it is that the human spirit rebels in the face of the palpable absurdity of the world (191) or with the words of Cavanaugh (121): " On February, 13th, Fr. Rutilio Grande of El Salvador gave a homily during Mass in the villa of Apopa.: The Lord gave us … a material world for all without borders…" A human world is a world of dialogue and exchange of humanity and also of all earthly goods. This is a concrete one not a universal (anonymous) Eucharist.

9. POLITICAL CRIME AND THE TRUTH OF A PERSON

Part one

Political crime

According to Ross (2003, 157) "the political crime is an important subject deserving investigation and explanation, and that a complete understanding can be achieved only when one appreciates the definitional issues, history, causes, and effects, is current, integrates cases, understands theory, and presents and evaluates relevant policy and practices."[3] The political crime is thus a very large term and includes several actions which are made by political power precisely by executing policy (governments) by the means of subordinate the citizens. The violation of the human rights should not be the primarily goal but there is always the first aim to maintain the political power and to exclude the potential rivals from the political parquet. So the purposes of such actions in the eyes of those politicians are 'to protect' or 'to preserve' the societal order but in many cases it means the protection of rule of leading power (nomenclature) of state.

It depends on the constitutional order of state, how political crime could be performed. Usually the democratic states are preserving the political order against attempts to bring disorder in the normal acting of states in the case with the terrorism. But there are several other political crimes "committed for the ideological purposes" (Hagen 1997, 3) and this crimes are "inspired by both ideology and the desire for personal benefit." (26) The leading power in these crimes is the secret police established specially by authoritarian regimes to protect the leading power. We can say that as the most strong, authoritarian is the regime much stronger is

3 Wikipedia defines the political crime in the following way: "In criminology, a political crime or political offence is an offence involving overt acts or omissions (where there is a duty to act), which prejudice the interests of the state, its government or the political system. It is to be distinguished from state crime when it is the states that break both their own criminal laws or public international law" (Political Crime, 21.2.2012). In our understanding the problem involves both: the ingress in the state sovereignty (by revolutionary acts) and the breaking of the laws and the human rights by totalitarian regimes.

the role and the power of the secret police: "In authoritarian regimes the effectiveness of secret police in deterring illegitimate violence (crime in the streets) occurs through legitimate secret police such as Hitler's Gestapo, Stalin's OGPU (later KGB), and Haiti's Tonton Macoutes…" (26) Hagan states that "the most dramatic examples of crimes by government is the pervasive international violation of human rights … Authoritarian and totalitarian regimes of the Left and Right are at least tolerant to political dissent and are thus the biggest violators" (28) There are different kind of these oppressions like performed by 'dead squads' (more countries of South America), 'murder unit' (South Africa), massacre (China 1990). The most cruel and mass murders are genocides performed by Turks against Armenians (1915-16), by Soviets, Nazis, Pol Pot Khmers Rouges, Serbs in Bosnia and Herzegovina (Srebrenica 1995), Hutu's in Rwanda (1994). All these are the tragic part of history of 20th century. The killings were performed with very sophisticated methods, propaganda and equipment of modern technique. The common goal of political crime is to exclude others which are the obstacle to the full political power of the one political group. This was the case not only by totalitarian regimes but by the groups trying to come to political power using all methods of political crime: terror, killing, laying to undermine the democratic orders in the societies. The communistic and other revolutions were the cruellest examples of the modern political crimes because they tried to work out the anthropological conversion of humans. According to Richard Pipes the communists played a leading role by the implementation of the criminal devices and methods (Pipes 1995) to establish the revolutionary state. We should see after an introduction in the modern rivalry, how it worked in Slovenian Case.

The societal exclusion as sideway

According to predominated anthropological and sociological theories the man is a complex being. So he can't be analysed, his identity of his inner and austere life remains open and never reached. Because of it he has to take himself as a mysterious being. This is for man as a reasonable being the problem, because he can't accept himself as an unknowable. "Very important is our attitude towards the question: Is the human being transcendent? … The awareness of transcendence questions is especially important in our age of outstanding, decided and conspicuous dominancy of the scientific form of consciousness." (Žalec 2002, 118)

So the complexity of man is expressed only by symbol; the eminent symbol is the human language. The partners of dialogue are needed to implement the dialogue and to reach this symbolic stage. The partnership is the necessary way to address the problem of secret of man and to go ahead to the mystery of human person. But the men as a free being can refuse the dialogue and suspend the others despite such refusals have negative consequences for him. The man can exclude or subordinate the others without to hear them and to accept their needs. This is the case in the interpersonal relations and much more difficulties bring it in broader socio-political relations if one group is up to exclude the others. If the societies couldn't reach a dialogical consensus, there is political disorder as the nutritious supposition for political crime as all revolutions and totalitarian regimes testifies (Hobsbawm 1996, Pipes 1995).

All oppressions were the consequences of exclusions of others who were victims of the usurpation of political power. This means that the language (dialogue) as a ground of mutual societal exchange was reduced only to one group of locutors who didn't allow the others to express their feelings and needs. Several exclusions include tendencies to reduce or to abolish the individuals and groups and to generalise their problems, which means to subordinate them under different ideas like nation, class or race. There is not easy to introduce the "model of pluralistic universalism" (Strahovnik 2009, 214), which respects the human person as condition and the subsidiary part of the wholeness.

Because of this the struggle for the truth is a tiresome way to the "universal ethic based on sense of the commonness of human experience. That misunderstanding (man as just scientific, isolated and without feelings, J. Juhant) of man has generated the wrong kinds of tensions between the full acknowledgement of the plurality of peoples and their cultures and the legitimate hopes for universal ethics, and, connected with that, between ethical truth and cultural determination of ethical value." (Gaita 2006, 284) According to Gaita it is very important to realise that the man is an imperfect being, a being that needs the others and is ready to acknowledge that he has been completed by them. Gaita (2006, 5) stresses that we have to deal with "preciousness of each individual human being". But he adds the sentence of Peter Winch, "a fine English philosopher", remarking "that 'treating a person justly involves treating with seriousness his own conception of himself, his own commitments and cares, his own understanding of his situation and of what the situation demands of him'." (Gaita 2006, 59)

The "ideal man" and rivalry

Because the man is a being of reason, as the Greeks said, but his knowledge is limited, this is the core problem. According to the Old Testament man's cognitive ambition is to "be like God." (Gen 3, 5) Because the man is not all-knowable God and his knowledge remains limited, the acknowledgment of this limitedness is a supposition for truth of the man. It is not in the first place a logical question but a moral one, the question of acknowledging his moral responsibility to others, which includes the will to divide the life with the other. The unwillingness to acknowledge this fundamental openness for truth of human reality is the cause and impediment to the knowledge of authenticity of human beings and thus the real humanity (Sloterdijk 2010, 135ff.). According to Sloterdijk, the Greek term *epistéme* testifies this openness for truths and confirms man's dialogical openness to the other and to the higher Good, God. But the modern economic and technological processes point out an ouster picture of 'ideal man', the man of technical perfection, which clauses the man's ability to be open for other.

Man of modern times was understood as a settled and scientific man, stimulating, guiding and governing the world and himself by science. He perceived himself as a big, strong man empowered by science and technique. They are the 'prolonged organs' of man. Man has a powerful sense of himself, which stimulated the faith that he would master the whole world. The historical and societal limitedness didn't and doesn't allow the people to get or to gain this ideal picture of man. Hannah Arendt (2005, 345ff.) in her work *The Origins of Totalitarianism* analyzed the history of the totalitarianisms of the 20th century as an usurpation of human rights because of implementation of this (reduced) picture of scientific-technical man. According to her and to Zygmund Bauman the holocaust couldn't be possible without all acquisitions of modernity. In the totalitarianisms only to the political adequate which means with the system congruent man was granted (reduced perfection) in contrast to others, who were excluded, diabolised and considered bad. The ideas of racism, nationalism, chosen classes and races, the 'better people' prevailed. Nietzsche was influenced by these modern tendencies and saw the solution in a strong, powerful man, who can pass the modern strong systems overruling them as a so called super-man. The revolutions and totalitarian systems implemented this agonal man, cleaning "all irregularities" to get the "clean' territories (Turkey in relation to Armenians; Serbs and Croats in relation to each other and to Bošnjaks). In all case there were intended that the ideal picture of clean people were the right man, other should not be human in full sense of this word. These facts are quit known but not clarified and in many cases there is a long way that the victims will become a satisfaction. This supposition of one-sided (wrong) picture of man was taken as a reason for justifying political crimes.

Mimetic theory

A contribution of the mimetic theory of Girard was to open the "anthropological constancy" of the rivalry. According to him the "just", the "other", the "weak" was chosen to be victimized and declared as guilty for bad conditions of society. Because he was innocent, he was made as a victim to be peacemaker and bearer of new relations in the society so that the society didn't need to change. In contrast to scientific picture of modern man René Girard (1989) wraps up the basic Judaeo-Christian topic of man: every man is a limited being, there is an "original sin", due to which there are not only bad or good, all are involved in victimisation and guilty. There are no class' enemies. It is not possible to exclude and not to see the breaches of human existence. Man is a *dividuum*, a divided being and thus imperfect being. To obtain this consciousness means to convert (*metanoia*) and be related to the other as a completeness of oneself. It means to be open for real relations to the other. Without this fundamental change in mind, which means to work on oneself, individual and societal reconciliation are not possible. Anybody could undertake to change his relations to others, but nobody can do it without acceptance of the other. This change begins in mind. If man is not ready to change his mind, he will persist in the (wrong) habits and customs he already has.

As said, the Greek term *epistéme* testifies a dialogical openness for truths and for the higher Good, God. But the modern processes point out an economically and technologically "ideal man", who could function perfect without deficits, despite these imperfectness and disorders are the fortune of the man on earth. This increases anger, dissatisfaction and unsolved tensions in individuals and in the society, and brings about a search for scapegoats, for the weak, who should help resolve "the mimetic crisis". The modern systems tried to get the perfect status of man through the political 'standardisations' and oppressions of individuals and groups. This caused several political crimes. The history of 20th century is full of sad examples beginning with Armenians, Jews, Gypsies, anticommunists and others victims from Nigeria to former Yugoslavia. The exclusion of many and the preferring of the "few" led to escalation of societal tensions. The victims were and still are the millions of poor people, dying of several deceases. The reasons are changes of global society, which causes the downfall of the traditional societal order and didn't provide the new rules and frameworks for the protections of individual. The process began with the establishing of new social class of workers, who were put on side of the society and the old classes wouldn't really accept them as a part of the society. This causes disturbances and revolutions. This continues in different forms until today. The victims of these processes are increasing over the world, still after the fall of communistic systems.

Truth of man and victimisation

According to René Girard's (2001) late work *I See Satan Fall like Lightning*, people every times supposed that victims are necessary and because of it they systematically designed frameworks to justify them. Despite this, we have today extensive (verbal) care for victims, yet we cannot be proud of such care. The criminal history of 20th century testifies that the readiness to cooperate and to reconciliation is far from the minimum to solve these complex problems of humankind. There are new and very fine methods to victimize the innocent. We should see only milliards of poor people condemned to starvation. After the end and fall of totalitarian regimes appeared new methods to victimize several groups and nations. Their number is still increasing. We are witnessing masses of victims, and there are many mechanisms by politics, media to conceal these crimes. We can paraphrase Girard (2001) by saying that the old myths were replaced by new (modern) ones as testifies the history of modern totalitarinisms and global media payers. Rivalries are taking place still now and the victims of this crisis of the humanity are increasingly enlarged. The consequence of this development is the exclusion of most people from the goods of this earth.

The human searching for truth has to take care for this very important dimension of truth of man today. As Girard (2001) it sees the prohibitions are made to protect the society from new outburst of violence. The victims are serving as mediators to overcome the tensions among the people. There are girls or boys sold for prostitution, for working or for terrorism that the clans could survive. Girard specially points out the violent danger of the sexuality: "All this regulations serve to endow both sexuality and violence with the same centrifugal force. In many instances the sacrificial deviations of sexuality and violence are virtually indistinguishable." (Girard 1979, 220)

The strongest, most influential desire, the sexual one, plays in these processes the leading role. The political crime is getting new faces and developing new finest methods. The modern women miss the human nearness and warmth; they are humanly not satisfied and rebel against the men, which open new tensions in the society.

The reason is an anthropological one. The wartime gives to men opportunity to show the power over the women, although otherwise they are dominated by the women. Secondly the warriors could perpetuate the dominance over the rivals through the raped women and conceived children, probably the future slaves. This performance should take place collectively and ritually that they become a sacred value – a sacred ware. It must happen in sacred rite and in a public ceremony. The performance is perfect if the tormenter succeed to persuade the victims to collaborate and to confess their guilt: "The mimetic collaboration of victims with their executioners continues in Middle Ages and even into our time…In our own times all forms of Stalinism find viperous victims who will confess far more than is asked of them…" (Girard 1989, 64)

All this dangerous processes and completed realities of man need the regulations and have a ritual and sacred dimension. So religions and rites took essential part on performing this task.

The rape is for the women not only violence but at the same time a treading down of their honesty. They lost their own homes and property; perhaps they become the child and were expelled from her relatives out of her communities. This is very usual in Islamic communities, despite it is not strange to other societies, because it is a question of the honesty of tribes respectively family-clans or nations, as it was example in the former Yugoslav wares.

To preserve the order in the society is a case too, if a woman, who was sexual abused by man, who commits adultery, should be stoned. She is a double victim: as well of sexual abuse as well of stoning. It would be necessary to investigate why it is better to offer the innocent woman instead the married man. Perhaps the marriage's institution should be preserved and therefore the woman should be offered. There are societies killing born girl to secure their survival. The women are supporting (participating on) this acts.

Part two

The modernity, violence and political crime - a Slovenian Case

After the World War I, the Slovenes were the part of Kingdom of Yugoslavia. The communists increased their societal actions in the multinational Yugoslav society, burdened by unsolved inter-national and societal problems. They recognised well the communistic methods in Soviet Union for taking power in the uncertain social environments. They were trained in Moscow to spread terror and to implement these methods at home. The circumstances like them in Russia during the World War I came in Slovenia in the World War II. The historians (Pipes 1995; Hobsbawm 1996) agree that the revolution in Russia couldn't take part without the World War II. The same was in the case in occupied Slovenia after 1941. When the Slovene communists in the first time after Nazis' occupation cooperated with occupiers (because of Pact Molotov-Ribbentrop 1940), after Hitler attacked the Soviet Union they began the revolution. Afterward with the sly tactic they began with 'left' Christian and liberal partners to establish *Osvobodilna fronta* (Liberation Front) which was the Trojan horse to execute the revolution in Slovenia. In the part of Slovenia under Italian fascist authority they began the revolutionary terror over the Slovenes. Several democrats especially Christians were executed. The situation was unbearable. For the repression the Italians killed the conscious Slovenes as hostages. Some of them were denunciated by communists. In the same way the Christians and democratic members of Liberation Front were executed if they didn't submit them under communistic power. The parish priests were killed and terrorised. Priest Jože Oražem on the conference of priests in Novo Mesto stated that the "the members of Liberation Front were propagating the mistaken principles and pursuing godless ideas…When this usurpers threatening the people in freedom, moving … then the physical self defensive is permitted ... to defend organized the villages and neighbourhood from unjust tyrants…" (Nadškofija 1942, F 37) At the dean-conferences of Ljubljana and Trebnje the priests stated numerous killing of priests and religious people: "Every shepherd of souls is acting as far as he can mostly for himself and in very limited work circle. There is no community. The both sadly assassinated priests couldn't be rightly buried; they still lie in the forest in grave excavated by themselves." (Nadškofija 1943, F 37)

After the World War II as the Slovene communist took power over the land they began to terrorized people. The victims were all Slovenes who opposed the communism. After the War the so called *domobranci* (home defenders), some with wives and children and other civilians, were given by the British to the Yugoslav communist and about 15000 people came to the communistic concentrations camps and in three months most of them were killed. Beside these Slovenes there were in Slovenia several groups from Croats, Serbian Chetniks and civilians without to be sentenced by courts killed. In the first years of communism several actual and virtual opponents, among them Christians and many priests, owners of enterprises, big farmers, etc. were expelled out of the country or killed. All people have to submit themselves under the political terror and pressure of the totalitarian dictatorships. In Slovenia there are near 1000 mass graves and many of them are still not investigated. There are over 100.000 people buried in them. There were several concentrations camp in Slovenia after the World War II for the adversaries of new regime, after the so called Resolution of Informbiro and the separation of Yugoslav Communist Party from Moscow in 1948 the communists of Yugoslavia established Goli otok, a settlement for their fictitious and real enemies.

Abnormal societal status

The ordinary people and experts agree that the communistic societal status was an abnormal. This is the case of all mimetic processes. The partisans of revolutionary methods can perform the crimes over the innocent victims only in an extraordinary status of society. The burdens of totalitarian regimes maintain and their totalitarian and criminal methods have a long duration. Afterword the people couldn't imagine in what kind of world they lived, the traditional values and virtues were replaced by vices like killing, laying, stealing. The soviet revolutionary methods of totalitarian oppression and subordination were repeated in Slovenia and in other communistic revolutionary circumstances. The communistic terror overflowed the societal life. The leading man of revolution Edvard Kardelj wrote to head of Yugoslav partisans Tito about the methods of so called "V*arnostno-obveščevalne službe" (Security-intelligence-service*; VOS) during the War: "…no security policy can save the denunciants, the hustlers of occupiers, who were targeted and caught by VOS … VOS is feared as a devil and this gives the *Liberation Front* - beside the *National Safeguard* and partisans – a character of really power." (Ferenc 1962, 325)

After the War the "real power" of terror's state was established in all pores of societal life. This was a stage of political terror. Nobody was safe and free. All people should come under control of communistic Party and secret police (force). The so called Yugoslav *self-regulatory-socialism* was a laying on potency because all decisions in the society were controlled and worked in all details by the leading communistic class. Because of it the system needed much more co-operators to control all participants of processes by the secret police. There were about half of population involved in this control system.

The special attention was given to the Catholic Church as a societal enemy nr. 1. Many priests were killed after the war at the prefabricated processes. Bishop Anton Vovk was attacked in the train on journey to Novo Mesto in January, 20th 1952. He was poured upon with gasoline and set on fire. He survived with life's consequences for his healthy. Among the Christians there were specially persecuted so called Christian socialist, who were the co-organisers of *Liberation Front* with the communist. Because the obedience among Slovenes was trained by Catholic Church and Austro-Hungarian Monarchy, the communist had much easier work to subordinate the Slovenes and to hold them in these unnatural circumstances. The totalitarian order in Slovenia and other totalitarian circumstances could be performed because of the obedient people, as Hanna Arendt and Zygmund Bauman stressed in mentioned works.

The revolutions of modernity couldn't happen without the capitalistic and general development of modern science and technique. They stimulated the modern system's thinking and the tendencies to subordinate people to perform the societal changes on account of the most poor people, who has to bear the great part of these changes. To do this the revolutionary circumstances should be introduced and the revolutionists were well trained to do it. Most of the revolutionary states were in un-order and the terrorist's attacks caused new un-order and provoked in the society the irregularly status. The society was brought to the new and new un-order and the measurement of government couldn't bring peaceful solutions like in Russia after 1900. Pipes (1995) worked out this unbearable status in the State of Russian tsar with a general hostility (hate) and unreadiness to cooperate. The first revolutionary acts are the nourishment for never ending revolution.

The Slovene communists imported these methods and implemented them in wartime 1941-1945. The propaganda machinery worked according to Lenin directive: "In my opinion it is necessary to use the capital punishment for all phases of plotting…" (Löw 1999, 241) The industrial development introduced great disproportions in the society and divided it and prepared the grounds for revolutions. Workers were the bearers of the 'modern development', but they get the least of its benefits. Peasants lost their base for survival. And this story is still not finished.

They are the modern slaves in new "democratic concentrations camps" not only in Guantanamo but in several other places of the world. The people given in then hadn't freedom to move, but are exploited for sex, work and other kinds of slavery (Kurz 2003, 180 ff.; Cacho 2011). Oedipus (the man) as a victim has become worldly – with global dimensions: from modern slaves at the beginning of modern times to workers, women and children as excluded classes of the society. Today this processes culminated in the status of global workers. The new political crimes are much more sophisticated. Many people are victims of luxuries of the modern consumer society: organised trade of modern slaves: women and children for prostitution, war and drugs (Cacho 2011). The modern Oedipus is entangled in the wealth of modern productive procedure, which produces masses of victims. This was the case of the genocide on Armenians, and other nations removal of "class enemies" by communist in several countries and groups like Palestinians until today. The political terror is still implemented over the Tibetans or peoples inhabit the Nuba Mountains, in Sudan, Africa; all these are still burning problems today. There are many signs that Christians in several Islamic countries are the tools of unsolved socio-political problems of their relation to the so called modernity.

The problem has nowadays global dimensions. The indolence of leaders and institutions of the society (governments, aristocracy, the new class of capitalists, churches) causes revolt of upper classes, peasants and workers, whose position is becoming more and more unbearable. Today these processes culminated in the status of global workers and other parts of society, what causes the problem of terrorism. More and more people are prisoners of these processes, this status is human abnormal and there are more and more of those modern consumer's victims: the majority of poor global masses, but especially starving people, children and (young) women exploited for prostitution, cheep work, wars and drugs. This unnatural status in the society is testifying by increasing problems of the society, the financial crisis. All these societal problems causes exploitation and crimes like trade of humans, organised prostitution, trade of arms and un-transparent financial streams.

The difficult way of reconciliation

The way to reconciliation and suspense of victimization is possible, because man has predispositions to good, but is very difficult and possible only by cultivation of dialogue (Ricoeur 2004, 491) and by the will for truth. Ricoeur mentions that in the "ultimate act of trust there is no recourse but to assume an ultimate paradox proposed by the Religions of Book" and which Ricoeur (2004, 490) finds "inscribed in the Abrahamic memory".

The human rights should be cultivated and protected for "lower people", who are all humiliated too. They have to take in account that their humanity should not be given up. It is very important to make the pedagogical and media campaign to persuade all people to take such care for themselves. Political and other rulers have to open and to explicate frameworks of the genocide of Armenians, the holocaust of Jews, other nations and groups, and removal of "class enemies". In Slovenia and everywhere else the process of reconciliation is as long and difficult process which presupposes a conversion of mind and readiness to cooperate. The logic of revolution of crime, which means lying, oppressing and exclusion, should be replaced by search for truth, freedom, cooperation … The latter are anthropological values, but to implement them we need steady willingness for dialogue at all levels of the society and in individuals.

There is a need for spiritual *metanoia*, which is a religious category, we need to combine the mystic and politics. Mystic is, according to Leonardo Boff (2011, 68ff.), the awareness that we all are children of God, who is our common father. He enables us to take all people as our brothers and sisters, not merely rivals. We need also the politics to work out the "kingdom of God" on earth. This utopia can work if we are always sincerely praying "Our father in haven", and we thus have the will to build his Kingdom on earth. This endeavour is very exciting without faith. The back side of the coin of human rights is the division of endeavour for humanity. It is impossible that only some people are bearers of the world's salvation. If we have faith in God, we have deeper reasons to see the truth and to bring reconciliation.

Raimond Gaita speaks about the "love to truth". "The deepest values of the life of the mind cannot be taught: they can only be shown, but, of course, only to those who have eyes to see." (Gaita 2006, 231). These eyes are eyes of heart. Mahatma Gandhi (1987, 134 ff.; 155ff.) stressed in this context the importance of the Christian teaching of Blessings. Gandhi made a synthesis of Indian sources of no-violence and Gospel's Sermon on the Mount (Blessings) of New Testament. The Blessings are a forgotten chapter of Christian's tradition. In short, the Spirit of Christ is a spirit of pure heart, of truth and justice, of non-possession and non-violence. There is no alternative to *metanoia*, to conversion of mind, if we want to get the changes in crisis of this world. These changes imply the changes in mind and the readiness to access to other empathically and dialogically. Despite this process there is maybe only utopia. There are no other chances for solving the problems of humans. There are reasons enough for humanity to be prepare for it and there are humans to be ready to undertake these processes and to help to change the direction of development of this world. The way will be, according to Strahovnik "a model of global ethics", as it worked out Robert Audi in *Moral Value and Human Diversity* (2007). "Audi combines (moral) virtue theories, Kantian ethics and utilitarianism and supplements them with moral intuitionism. Virtue theories focus on 'being a good person', developing virtues that constitute good life and happiness, and subsequently try to work out what the conduct must be like in relation to that kind of virtuous person. Kantian ethics focuses more on rules or a moral law one must follow in order to pursue the right thing. Respect and dignity of a person are important here. Utilitarianism is also a rule-based moral theory, but one which evaluates act in relation to their consequences, especially regarding well-being, happiness and reducing suffering of persons and community as a whole." (Strahovnik 2009, 215)

The Christian tradition worked out this respect to the dignity of human person in the discussions about the personality of Jesus Christ on the first Christian councils, where the human person was discussed as grounded in God. According to this the most influent tradition of the human history of last two thousand years was inspired by this transcendent personalism. "Transcendent personalism provides good reasons to tolerate many other and different views." (Žalec 2011, 113) The respectful behaviour needs profound sources. The conversion to dialogue and to partnership can take place only (using Plato's diction) by memory of the eidetic world. So the respect of the Charter of Human Rights or to practice the universal morality is possible only by supposition of *orthos logos* (the right reason). The *metanoia* (change in mind) as a Christian universalistic term is not applicable in the present secular society, which thinks in racial categories (Ocvirk 2012). To make a decision for a non-violent behaviour towards others and to respect full the rights of every living being, the man needs faith and hope. This faith is grounded on the supposition of a deeper insight into the reality, which is usually understood as a religious act known in different way in several religious and other traditions.

If there were in the past (for modernity) religious rules and rites to secure the societal order and to prevent the escalations of the violence, this is no more the case of today. The individual is lost in the open global circumstances, in which ways of political crime of groups, nomenclatures and state's oligarchies are open. The new world and socio-political order doesn't provide the individual to react to this complex situation. Because of it the individual is a victim of these processes. The post-modern man is more and more lost in the global world, a world without of rites of behaving. The Nietzschean ideal of man could and should be universalized in sense that all people are invited to realise the moral ideal of man. But this is not a man of technique, science, political (totalitarian) or consumer system, but only a human man. Because of it the solution could not be reached in this world. There is no "hyper-policy" (Zimmermann 2008, 157), the instrument of regulating this is no totalitarian system, no classless society, no world policy. This means, that there is not a all pervading formula to reach the human order, there is only the struggeling interpersonal dialogical way. This can be followed by dialogue among man and the man with God, in truth and love.

APPENDIX: SLOVENIAN THEOLOGY

Basic facts: Population (number, ethnic differentiation)

Slovenia is the most western nation among the Slavic nations and located at the important geographical crossing between Romanic, Slavic and German nations. Slovenes have thus had to provide for their survival under the pressure of Germans and Romans. Christianity came to Slovenia from Aquileia and Salzburg through Irish-Scottish monks. The Germans in particular hindered the autonomy of the Slovene people and thus prevented the missionary work of Cyril and Methodius, imprisoning Methodius in Ellwangen (Germany), because they sought to exploit the missionary work for imperial purposes. As a result, the Slovene people had to establish their political framework within the Austro-Hungarian Monarchy.

The time of national growth deepened the pressure of the dominant nations of Germany and Austria on other nations. Slovenes, Croats, Serbs in the South and the Czechs and Slovaks in the East decided during the First World War to separate themselves from the Austro-Hungarian Monarchy. The Slovene politicians Janez Evangelist Krek (1865-1917), Anton Korošec (1872-1940) and others worked toward the separation of these nations and their subsequent reunion with the Serbian Monarchy in the Monarchy of Serbs, Croats and Slovenes, later as the Kingdom of (First) Yugoslavia (1918). The new state could not solve the problem of nationalism and the leading nation, Serbs, oppressed the other nations so that the state could fall. Around this time, the king Alexander Karađorđević was in October 9th 1934 in Marseille assassinated and up to the Second World War the political situation in state was going worse and worse because national and social tensions and growing pressure of Yugoslav communists, who tried to exploit these circumstances for their revolutionary purposes.

The communist revolution occurred during and was fulfilled after the Second World War. There are about 46,000 victims of the revolution in Slovenia. Already in the year 1942, about 1000 prominent catholic or democratic civilians and opponents of revolutionary methods were killed by communists' executive policy. Again after the war there were about 15,000 Slovene people killed by the communists. Because of its geographical situation the Slovene area was the location of the mass-killing of all of the anti-communist populace of Yugoslavia. The communists called "collaborators of the occupiers", many of them, civilians, - about 150,000 people: Germans, Croats, Serbian Chetniks and members of other nations fled to the West. Most of them were captured by the communists; some of them were given by the western (Anglo-American) troops to the communists because of the Teheran agreement (November 28th – December 1st 1943) between Anglo-Americans and Soviets. About 20,000 Slovenes emigrated to Italy, Austria, USA, Canada and Argentina.

During the communist period, the Catholic Church was controlled and suppressed. Many Catholic priests and laymen were imprisoned and some of them were killed. The migrations, executions and oppression were mostly inflicted on the Catholic population, so that the "quality" of population changed evidently. This means that the public life afterwards was directed in a "revolutionary manner". In the words of Berdjajew (1979), the communist man was a rough man, a man of violence. It also meant that Catholic resp. democratic societal values, sensibilities and mentality were dispelled from the public life, and could only be cultivated privately. The revolutionary logic prevailed.

The changes of 1989 brought about formal democracy but the communists remained in major positions of society and they still significantly direct public life until now (2013). The Slovenes had their own state and thus formally, they were free to decide about their own lives. The believers could practise their religion, but they had to fight with the repercussions of the long communist era. There was no lustration in the Churches and States institutions.

Slovenia and Catholicism

Traditionally, the main religion in Slovenia has been Catholicism. There are about 1.8 million Catholics (about 82 % - Slovenia has about 2 million people). The second major religion is Islam. There are about 2.4 % Muslims and about 2.3 % Orthodox Christians and 0.8 % (autochthon) Protestants. Protestants were very important for the Slovene language, because they wrote the first Slovene books. Although Slovenes have some older religious documents in Slovene language (Brižinski spomeniki, about 972 and 1039) in Zgornja Koroška (Upper Carinthia): General confession, Preaching about Sin and Penance). The first Slovene books were published by Protestants. With the translation of the Bible into Slovene (Jurij Dalmatin, 1547-1589) and with other religious texts like the Catechism, the Protestants established thc Slovene written language. Because the Slovene region was under the governance of Habsburg House, the most of Slovenes had to remain Catholic. Only in the North-East was there a Protestant aristocracy and there, Protestantism remained.

Orthodox Christians came to Slovenia from Serbia and Bosnia, while Muslims came from Bosnia and Kosovo. Many of them came to Slovenia as so called "guest-workers", some of them as refugees in the time of wars in Bosnia and in Kosovo. Most of them now have Slovene citizenship.

As many other former communist countries, Slovenia has a very liberal policy towards other religions, but under the governance of the former communists the Catholic faith was still treated with disdain.

Faculty of Theology in Slovenia

Slovenia has four university centres: Ljubljana, Maribor and (new) Koper, near Trieste and (new) Nova Gorica. There is one Faculty of Theology in Slovenia; it has two departments. The main center is in Ljubljana, because the faculty is the member of the University of Ljubljana. The department in Maribor has only two programs, not incorporated in the University of Maribor, but as a part of the University of Ljubljana: Bologna program three years diploma (baccalaureate) *Theological and Religious Studies*, Bologna Master program Studies *Family and Marriage Therapy* and Combinatory program with the university Maribor.

Both departments had about 500 students yearly, the number is going down. Among them 66% are women, and there are about 40 candidates for the priesthood. It is surprising that students are so interested in theology, as this education does not offer many possibilities for jobs. One reason for this is that the other faculties of humanities and social sciences are not ready to open free research and educational programs.

The faculty has also several (Bologna) programs: Program of *Theology* (-5 years) with the university master degree of theology, an interdisciplinary program in combination with the faculty of Arts in

Ljubljana and with the three faculties of Maribor, program "*Theological and Religious Studies*" (three years). Then the master program "*Religiology and Ethics*" and master program "Marriage and Family Therapy Studies".

The first program, the regular study of theology, is intended for candidates for the priesthood but can also be undertaken by lay persons. Lay persons undertaking this course of study often have difficulty obtaining employment, particularly in the area of teaching. In Slovenia, there are neither Catholic religious lessons nor any kind of religious teaching in schools. There is a choice-program of *Religion and Ethics* in the last three years of the Nine-Year Primary School, but pupils can choose among the following subjects: Religion and Ethics, Rhetoric, and second foreign language. Few students end up choosing *Religion and Ethics*.

The program is combined with other disciplines. In Ljubljana it is a combination of Theology and some subjects on the Faculty of Arts (Philosophy, History, Languages, and so on), while in Maribor it is a combination of Theology and disciplines with the Faculty of Education, Faculty of Arts and Faculty of Natural Sciences and Mathematics of the University of Maribor. The program takes four years and these graduates can more easily get a job in schools.

It was very difficult to renew the programs through Bologna's Declaration. Neither the Church's authorities nor professors were ready to accept the new university degrees with a three years bachelor degree. With Master of theology we could reach an agreement in these dilemmas.

Slovenia has now one bishop-seminary for all Slovene dioceses'. After the financial bankruptcy of dioceses Maribor there is impossible to hold there any economic institution. There are also some religious-seminaries of Franciscans, Minorits, Capucins, Salesians, Jesuits, Congregation of Missionaries and Cistercians all candidates study at the Faculty of Theology in Ljubljana. There are about 40 seminarians studying with the faculty in Ljubljana and some sisters of women' communities.

During the communist era there were two minor seminaries with their own (private) high schools, and seminary in which the seminarians went to the state high school. Now there are four high schools of dioceses of Ljubljana, Koper, Maribor and one, of the Salesian Congregation, in Želimlje as regular high schools with state concession and with both men and women scholars. Slovenia has now four high schools of this kind. Although there are no seminarians in these high schools, they are very important places of Catholic education. We have some kindergartens with the concession and one catholic primary school.

The Faculty of Theology in the former Yugoslavia was a very important ecumenical institution. It organized ecumenical meetings between Serbian Orthodox, Croat Catholic and Slovene Catholic theologians. These meetings were an important place of ecumenical exchange. The theologians from the Ljubljana Faculty played the leading role in this discussion, a cause they were not burdened from national and cultural prejudices. Slovene theologians have a long tradition in ecumenical work. France Grivec (1878–1963) was the leading ecumenical theologian in the area of Middle Europe. In the time between the two World Wars he organized the ecumenical congresses in Velegrad (Chechoslovakia (Grivec 1960). From the role of Cyril and Methodius he stressed the necessity of a new ecumenical movement and he prepared the ideas of the Second Vatican Council. He spoke in his works about the spirit of the new profound and brotherly spirit of the ecumenical Christianity, which should bind the orthodox and Catholic Christians. The communist period broke with this tradition, but because the communists supported the Serbian Orthodox Church as a national church, they were interested in this form of dialogue. In this way they were able to promote their political image as liberal communists. Now the department of Theology of University of Ljubljana in Maribor will proceed with this ecumenical work.

The history of theology and theological teaching

Because Slovenes have not had their own state since the early Middle Ages, the Catholic Church was the main institution which has protected, guided and kept Slovene's temper. Slovenes depend on the Church. They also fear the representatives of the Catholic Church--priests. There is a Slovene saying: "You should take a priest only for salt." Despite this, priests and bishops were for a long time the only intellectuals in the Slovene nation. They worked not only for religious purposes, but also for cultural, economic, social and political affairs of Slovenes.

Theologians in particular were the first politicians, agricultural educators, social workers and cultural awakeners of the nation. This role was especially important in the time when the Slovene national consciousness began. The neoscholastic movement in Slovene regions in the Austro-Hungarian monarchy was not only a philosophical revival but a mass national movement. The Catholic national movement at the end of the 19th century contributed to the political, cultural, social and economic programs for the development of the Slovene nation. Janez Evngelist Krek (1865–1917), bishop Anton Bonaventura Jeglič (1850–1937), Anton Korošec (1892–1940), Aleš Ušeničnik (1868–1952), and other theologians and priests guided this work. Catholic theologians played an important role in the advancement of the national and political independence of the Slovene people. In the 1920s, Catholics in Slovenia like those in some other countries of Europe tried to find a more spiritual Catholicism and in doing this, they differentiated themselves. A very important group was the one of Crusades, who played an important role in the Slovene Liberation Front. They helped communists to take power over the Slovene nation and to achieve the revolution.

After the revolution at the end of the Second World War, the communists began their fight against the Catholic Church and religion. The influence of this fight against religion and the Church still remains in the phase of the so-called transition.

It is very important to stress that in speaking about theology in Slovenia and in other post-communist countries it should be assumed that:

1. The Christian tradition of faith in these countries has been rapidly fragmented by the new societal situation. The transition has brought about sudden changes in religious attitude. Freedom makes possible a free religious practice, but also a quick extirpation of traditional religious habits which were during the communist era violently driven out of societal consciousness. Now people can live freely and they can decide freely regarding religious questions too, but they have because of former communistic time no so much religious socialisation especially about public use of religion. This is so more complicated situation we have in the western countries with a longer democratic tradition (Fukuyama 2000), because the process there was more organic. Because of this, the task of the theologians of these countries is to deal with the problems of a postmodern and post-communist society (Juhant 2005). It is necessary to involve in this work sociologists and psychologists and to cultivate an interreligious dialogue, which has been traditionally a theological task (Feiner 1965).

2. Through the changes in the transition, a new discussion about the role of the religion in society took part. In Slovenia this discussion was opened in the twenties and thirties of the 20th century through a new spiritual movement in the Catholic Church. Communism stopped all discussions about the role of the religion in a society, and Christendom was pushed to the sacristy. There was no possible to discus and to write about these problems. Only members of the Cyril-Methodius Society could write under control of the communist authorities.

3. So the publications of these theologians were self-censored. Theologians by themselves had to take care that they didn't write about themes or problems that the communists did not agree with. This is true also for ethical-religious issues. Theologians had to control their statements, in order to avoid making the communist leaders angry. The *Cyril-Methodius Society* in particular was remunerated for its loyalty to the communist authorities (Juhant, Potočnik 2001)[4]. Because of this, theology was mutilated. It was pushed into certain narrow societal passageways and it could not really openly address the relevant societal or political questions of believers. This was the fate of the so called "*Contextual-Theology*" of auxiliary bishop Vekoslav Grmič (1923–2005) from Maribor. He proclaimed this theology as a theology of self-governance and wanted to stress that the state communist system of self-governance had theological implications. But the Yugoslav system of self-governance was a communist trick to gain more control over the citizens. In this manner bishop Grmič gave support to the system of secret police. In his theology, bishop Grmič criticised the hierarchical structure and the authoritative style of the Catholic Church but he did not say anything critical about the state communist system. When questioned about this, he answered that he is not competent to criticise the state but only the Church's authorities.[5] The contextuality of the theology of self-governance was only an ideological help for the communist system. As a result the Yugoslav system was because of its system of "self-governance" the most cunning of all the communist systems. The position

---

4 The Society was founded on September 1, 1949 with the intention that the communist leaders would control the Catholic Church. Society members could collect money from the Catholics, they could avail themselves of social security and they could obtain the old age pension insurance.

5 The bishop personally said this sentence to the author during the communist times.

of theologians was very difficult and it left consequences also in the time of transition.

The Faculty of Theology and its role in society

The Faculty of Theology contributed, along with other main faculties (Philosophy, Law, Medicine, Technical Sciences), to the foundation of the University of Ljubljana. The Jesuits founded in 1619 in Ljubljana a department of theology and as a result the University of Ljubljana recognizes this date as the beginning of the university studies in Ljubljana. The study of theology continued until December 1919, when the University was founded. Theologians also had an important role in the foundation of the Slovene Academy of Sciences and Arts. The philosopher and theologian Aleš Ušenicnik (1868–1952) was the head of the Initiative Committee of the founders of the Academy (1938). He was for more than fifty years the leading person of Slovene Catholics and of the whole Slovene nation. He was a member of the Pope Romane Academy St. Thomas of Aquinas in Rome.

There was also a theological high school in Maribor until 1941.

After the revolution in the year 1949 the Faculty of Theology was excluded from the University of Ljubljana. The High School in Maribor was cancelled. With the decree dated by the authors June 31st (!), the Faculty of Theology from Ljubljana was declared a private Church institution. In May of 1991 the Faculty regained its status as a state institution and on 18 November 1992, it was reintegrated in the University of Ljubljana. The University declared the habilitations on the faculty members were in conformity with the university policy on habilitations. The professors started to get regular salaries – they were very small at the times when the faculty was only a church institution and it was very difficult to work without books. Henceforth professors could take part on the competitions of the Ministry for High School, Science and Sport for science researches. The students of theology received a regular status as students - acknowledged by the state.

The Faculty of Theology now has again full authority at the University. This means that all regular procedures: habilitations, research, teaching, and examinations with all regulation in relation to the students is hold by the University and the theologians have to take part on them. The Church has a great chancellor and professors have to be approved before the habilitation by him. But this is a practical solution and there is no legal regulation between the State and the Church in this matter. Because there is only a formal agreement between the Holy See and the Republic of Slovenia about the status of the Catholic Church in our society, most problems of this relation are open. Slovenia has no religious lessons in schools, there is a hospital care of souls but it is not paid by hospitals or by the state. There are many other questions to be solved.

After the Faculty of Theology was reintegrated in the University of Ljubljana it gained many students. Because there are no religious lessons in grammar schools and it is difficult for these students to procure employment. There is still a negative attitude in the society toward religion and consequently against theology. The Faculty of Theology was often declared as a Trojan Horse of the Church so that the Catholic religion can seek influence in society.

A new situation is the integration of Slovenia into European Union. Slovenes now have new courage and these changes have been echoed in the larger society even the societal problems of transition and the influence of former communist on main sectors of societal life remained, which make more and more difficult the improvement of the societal life.

A new challenge for theology in the university was the process of Bologna. It renewed all programs and developed a new framework for teaching at the university a new framework, a new pedagogy, and reorganized program for the achievement of the diploma. It is helpful that the Holy See arranged for those studying theology in institutions in the EU to earn a master's degree. This solution has been arranged for the study of medicine too (without three additional years of study for a bachelor's degree).

It is very difficult to change the mentality of the professors and to adapt them to the new mode of teaching. Theologians are stretched between the care for the integrity of the discipline and the new issues brought about by changes to the global society. In the transitional society of Slovenia, theology has taken a part in the societal changes as well.

There were some tensions between biblical and philosophical contents in the curricula. Professors of the Bible are convinced that the biblical contents are the decisive contents of the theological study. Professors of philosophical subjects call person's attention on the hermeneutical process of the word of God, which requires good knowledge of philosophical, psychological, and sociological conditions of man. The Congregation for Catholic Education in its *Decree on the Reform of Ecclesiastical Studies of Philosophy* from January 28th, 2011 confirmed the meaning of philosophy for theological study. It is very important especially in the post-communist countries. People here do not have enough hermeneutical experience, because they were systematically trained not to think but only to obey. For the same reason it is very important that all theological disciplines are open to the problems of time and space. The Slovene theologians are not ready enough to open their thoughts to real problems of the postmodern person. They take very important changes in our society slowly by transition from the communist system to democracy, and by the challenge of globalization. But they are not alone. Theologians in the world Christian church also have difficulties on this matter.

There is also a problem with the relation between theologians and the church authorities. There are not any troubles between the Slovene theologians and the Slovene Church authorities. But there are not so many viewpoints regarding how to deal with the problems of the postmodern person. Some professors have no idea what theology should do in this situation. On one side, they stress that theology has to be ecclesiastical and should obey and observe all orders of Rome. But on the other side they are prepared to cooperate with different political, economic and other powers to attain more influence in the society. The faculty has not made any common statement concerning the real societal and ecclesiastical problems of the Slovene Church. They do not have any opinion of lay men and women. The Slovene Church synod gathered some opinions about this area but it has not opened the discussion about the real problems of the Church in our society. The synod has not developed a strategy concerning the Church's approach to the problems of our society. Because there are many students of theology, they will require new decisions about the role of theology in the society and in the Church.

Reception of the Vatican Council

In the communist era, the main event for Slovene Catholics was, besides the Protocol-Holy-Seat-Yugoslavia (June, 25th 1966), the Second Vatican Council (1962-1965). In the former communist countries it was difficult for bishops to get permission from the authorities of the state to take a part on the Council. Bishops were also instructed, as to what they should say at the Council. Most of the communist states didn't give the permission to all bishops. The communist leaders decided it with the motto "Divide et impera !" They only permitted some bishops to go to the Council. "The most general characteristic of the participation of the bishops from the communist countries on the Council was the limited freedom through the decisive role of the politics of communist rulers... It is a historical question, how the bishops of the other so called 'free countries' could realize this problem of the freedom of the bishops from the 'iron curtain'. The affected Churches have after the political change now to decide this question of the real freedom in the Church and in the society." (Máté-Toth 2001, 334) The problem of 'self-limitedness of theology has to be solved by theologians of the former communist countries.

All Slovene ordinaries received permission to go to Rome. In turn, they all signed the declaration against the condemnation of the communist system (Acta Synodalia sacrosancti Concilii Oecumenici Vaticani II 1977, 804-805).

The Slovene Church was well informed about the events on the Council (Lah 2001, 9-31).[6] The news came through the Vatican radio; the Church newspaper *Družina* was informed by the agencies from abroad about the events at the Council too. There were bulletins of by the state-organized society of the Catholic Priests Nova pot (New Way). In particular, the professor of theology Stanko Canjkar (1900–1977) wrote regularly his estimations and statements about the events of the Council. He stressed the different streams of the Council. Because of the influence of this theologian on the Constitution about the Church in the Present World this document was very welcomed by the Slovene Church. It was widely appreciated that for the first time women could participate on the Council (Lah 1964, 161). Družina wrote that the Council with this Constitution confirmed its raison d'etre (Lah 1964, 185). It presented the main themes of the Constitution (Lah 1964, 185-192). *Družina* reported: "With this

---

6 The foundation of my thesis at this point represents the valuable research of my colleague Avguštin Lah entitled Sprejem 2. vatikanskega koncila v Sloveniji (The Reception of the Second Vatican Council in Slovenia). He prepared the following four quotations from *Družina*. I am giving him many thanks for this.

Constitution the main conclusion of the Council was realized." (Lah 1964, 246-247) The Slovene Church presented the new ideas of the Council despite its difficult situation.

It was, however, very difficult to promote these ideas in the daily life of the Church in Slovenia. The communists closely controlled the life of the Church and they were not prepared to allow free thinking. The best example is the professor of spiritual theology of Gregoriana Jesuit Vladimir Truhlar (1912-1977). He decided to return to Slovenia. As an open-minded theologian who especially stressed the meaning of the theological spiritual experience[7] and who sometimes criticized the Church's authorities, he was very welcomed by the communists. He wrote two interesting books about the Council *Post-council catholic ethos (Pokoncilski katoliški etos*- Truhlar 1967) and Catholicism in the process of deepening (*Katolicizem v poglobitvenem procesu* - Truhlar 1971). These books had a very important influence, especially among Catholic and liberal intellectuals. In his books he stressed the important role of laity in the Church and he argued for the synodal principle in the Church. He tried to implement these ideas in the Catholic Church of Slovenia, but the communists worried about this project and they prevented him from being influential. He ultimately went abroad again and died in Südtirol (North Italy). Truhlar pointed out the problem of freedom of theological thinking, while he stressed the spiritual experience of faith like Karl Rahner. But this free experience pleased neither the Catholics nor the communists. Theologians criticized the openness of the theological system because for them, faith through too much experience would not be objective enough. The communists saw in this theological openness a potential danger for their rigid totalitarian system.

There were other theologians who tried to combine communism and Catholic theology. It was a question of survival to find ways of cooperation. The philosopher Janez Janžekovič pointed out the immense role of ethics as a bond between Marxism and Christianity (Juhant 2002, 51-53). He thought that a socialist system (like it was the Yugoslav communism) was much better than the capitalist one (Juhant 2002, 54). The communist teaching about the equality of all people was estimated by him as a common ground of meeting for Christians and Marxists. The

7 In 1974 Truhlar´s *Leksikon duhovnosti* (*Lexicon of Spirituality*) was published, which was translated in several languages.

goal of ethics--to reach the good life--should be in the same sense the ground of socialism. "Our enemy is not socialism but only atheism." (Janžekovič 1978, 148) But the communists understood that the theologians had to subordinate themselves. They could use only limited freedom, and they had to accept the totalitarian order of the society. It was the time of the so called "dialogues"[8]. (Garaudy, Metz, Rahner 1970, 29) But the communist authorities of the Marxist states understood it differently than the Christian thinkers. If J. B. Metz wrote about "the public responsibility of the Christian faith in the society" (Garaudy, Metz, Rahner 1970, 138), the communist dictators did not allow any public manifestations of Christianity. But through Christian comprehension, theology has to take the responsibility of social situation. It was important in the communist times – even though it was very difficult – and it is very important in the postmodern secular society. It is the problem of freedom of theology and its covenant to the situation of people as it is pointed out at the beginning of the Constitution of the Church in the contemporary world: "The joys and the hopes, the griefs and the anxieties of the men of this age, especially those who are poor or in any way afflicted, these are the joys and hopes, the grieves and anxieties of the followers of Christ." (Pastoral Constitution of the Church in the Modern World=GS 1966, 199-200) This task cannot be performed, if theology doesn't understand itself as a symbolic theology, as Rahner says (Rahner 1961, 278. 291). To be open for the otherness of the world it means for the otherness of man. It is impossible in a closed dictatorial society. Theology should not be lost in any system. But it is a problem of Catholics, because they were trained in obedience through the system of the Church. Like Zygmund Bauman says, obedience is the problem of education in a rigorist system (Bauman 2002).

Freedom and the condition of theology in transition

The main problem of theology is the problem of freedom. The former communist countries have "the unhappy gift of freedom." (Josef Tischner: Biel 1996, 171) The pressure of the communist regime made people unreceptive to an open use of freedom. The socialistic person has been trained hierarchically, centrally and authoritatively. The main

---

8 Roger Garaudy derived the possibility of the dialogue between Marxism and Christianity from the Council.

authority was the secret police. The political leaders gave themselves the right to decide about the lives of their citizens. Through the secret police, the party had control over the lives of citizens. It was very important that all citizens were under complete control (Arendt 1979, 693). The party held especially strong control over the Church and the believers. They had some priests as collaborators, because they compelled them with their methods of pressure to work with the secret police. It was not so difficult, because the Church's hierarchical system is a good foundation for this dialectic of order, as Zygmund Bauman says. The Exilslovene Dušan Lajovic, living in Australia, published a list of Slovenes who were controlled or who as collaborators of the secret police controlled other citizens. There were 1,000,000 Slovenes (fully half of the population) involved in the web of control (Lajovic 2001). But it is an anomaly of post-communist society of Slovenia that the plaintiff accused the publisher, instead of accusing some of the former collaborators of the secret police. It has opened a heated discussion about the rights of the persons on the list and the rights of the people who were prosecuted.

The problem of the Slovene post-communist society is that the influence of this secret web is so strong that nobody involved in it is prepared to speak about these connections. The problem is that there are clerics involved in this web and some of them are now collaborating with the transitory communists. As a result, the relations between the citizens are not made clear. Citizens are afraid because there are old connections and the former communists have still societal power until to the year 2013. The situation changed with the entrance of Slovenia in the European Union in a sense that the control of financial and economic life is possible from European institutions. Despite this it is still difficult not to know who were - or still are – collaborators with the communist leaders.

Because of it the wrongs have not been solved, and those people who were victims of the communist regime are still victims of it, even though they are in a formally democratic state. It is very difficult to free people from the clasp of communism. The reason for this is that the former communists not only in Slovenia, but in other countries as well, still have much power in society. Jože Pučnik was the head of the parliamentary commission for the Investigation of the Revolutionary Processes off Law and Mass Killings. He found out that the relatives of victims and the causers were not prepared to speak about this. (Pučnik 2003) There is an agreement between old communists not to say anything about these events.

It makes difficult to speak about the truths in the society and also in the Church, if these relations are not clear. So it is very difficult to speak about freedom in theology, if theologians are not ready to clear their positions. The synod of the Church of Slovenia added nothing to solution of this question. But without this the conclusions of the synod will remain only on a paper (Tajništvo sinode Cerkve na Slovenskem[9] 2000). The Church didn't say the last word in this processes and it could not pose the strategy for its work in the future. Theologians couldn't dialogize about their role in these processes and so they couldn't help the Church to reach the full freedom and to help to free other citizens.

A problematic position of religion and theology in a transitional society

The Chair of Philosophy and of the Institute of Christian Philosophy and Ethics on the Faculty, the author of this article, has completed in the last years much research and has organized symposia about this complex Slovene history. He published 16 volumes about the relevant questions of our history, particularly of our Christian tradition. (Juhant 1997; Juhant, Potočnik 2002, 51-53; Jamnik 1998) He began his studies on Georg Hermes and on the problem of the relation of modernity and Christianity from Kant until the Marxist period (Juhant 1978). There were established the Institutes of Religion, of Ecumenism and Dialogue, of History, of Moral Theology and the Spiritual Questions of the Time and two programs paid by the Ministry for High School, Sciences and Technology. Through this we have investigated the fundamentals of the Christian culture in our tradition. During 50 years of communism the Christian roots of our culture were negated. It is a question of rightness to give stress to this heritage. The second motif was the search for Christian values in our society. It is the question, if, how and what kind of role do Christian values have after 50 years of communism, which tried to expel the Christian tradition out of our society? It is combined with the question of our national identity. We worked this topic out in several publications. The problem of national identity and its combination with the

9 Secretary of the Synod in Slovenia.

collectiveness of Christendom in Slovenia is influenced by the Marxist conquest of Slovenia. It remains an open question of Slovene history and especially of the Slovene history of Christianity.

The author of this article published as a result of the project "The Sense and Value of Religions," a book with the same title (Juhant 2000). It is the work of a theologian investigating the topic of religion. There are also "investigations" of religion by Slovene sociologist, but these sociologists are Slovene Marxist sociologists. And this is a problem. In the communist times the so called "sociologists of religion" dealt with religion in order to expel it out of society. They played a very important role as assistants of the former communists supporting their continued dominance on the top of the post-communist society. They proclaimed religion as harmful for society and worked out a program to dispel it out of society. They had the full organizational support of the communist leaders to fulfil this task. It is very interesting and understandable that the leading Marxist sociologist Zdenko Roter, a colonel of the secret police, was the main interrogator especially of priests who were jailed. This group of sociologists made with their own methods and with the support of the communist politicians and political ideology that believers felt inferior in the society. Because of it they kept their political role in the time of transition. People are still afraid to show their new societal relations. It was decisive that the transitional communists could retain their political role in the society after the changes, too. They organized a political and electoral campaign for the former communist leaders. One of them, sociologist Niko Toš, guided the public opinion centre and tried to adapt the public opinion so to make benefit for the former communist party. As a head of the Institute for the Public Opinion he is a close collaborator of the post-communist nomenclature. It also helped that the former communists carried out the privatization to their advantage. This group of sociologists, with professors of other professions, indoctrinated students and by using the media the whole Slovene society. They especially tried to retain the role of Catholicism in the society in the framework of the communist era, which is private and isolated. This ideological role has been seriously questioned since Slovenia has joined the European Union.

Present work of Slovene theologians

The tenured professor of philosophy, Janez Juhant, has written books about the Slovene social-political history, the history of philosophy as well as a book on anthropology (Juhant 2001, Juhant 2003). He published an anthology of faculty contributors entitled "*Theology in the rupture of the time*" (Juhant [ed.] 2000) Presented in this anthology are the problems of the individual theological branches in the relation to problems of the society of transition. The author presented that theologians could not sufficiently realize the burning problems of theology at this time. Theologians in Slovenia and over the world do not pay adequate attention to this topic. Juhant's book *Globalisation, Church and Postmodern Man* deals with the principal question: Has the Church anything to say to the postmodern person? Changes in society are so deep and so tectonic that society needs a new approach (Juhant 2005). Priests are narrow passageways between the postmodern democratic and individual world, and the hierarchical structure of the Church. The Church has to decide if it is prepared to descend from its lofty pulpit and willing to accept the reality of the postmodern individual person. Juhant's research program deals with values of individualism and the possibility of attaining social capital for the life of society and the Church. The research group investigated the possibility of implementation of values in societal and pedagogical processes in Slovenia and throughout the world. The primary goal is to implement conditions for dialogue in the local and global world. Eight scientific monographs regarding these topics were published at publishing house LIT.

One part of Slovene theology and religious philosophy was significantly shaped by a Slovene torrent of Brentano´s or Meinong´s stream in philosophy. Its main representative France Veber (or Weber) (1890-1975) started as a succesful pupil of Meinong in Graz. In 1920 he started his career at the University of Ljubljana and became the first professor of philosophy at the Faculty of Arts in Ljubljana. Until 1945, when the communists came to power he was, together with Ušeničnik, the foremost proponent of Slovene philosophy and was extremely popular. Afterwards it was dangerous to discuss his philosophy and consequently it was forgotten. Later Weber developed a philosophy strongly oriented in the same direction as the Christian religion (Weber 1923; 1934; 1954). Weber passed on 23 doctors of philosophy (PhD) to Slovene science, and strongly influenced such important thinkers as Anton Trstenjak (1906–1996, his PhD topic in Innsbruck [1928] was Weber´s ethics). The most faithful developer of Weber´s thought is Ludovik Bartelj (1913–2006), who lived as a priest at Dole pri Litiji and who earned his PhD in theology at the Faculty of Theology in Ljubljana in 1973. Bartelj published eleven philosophical books in which he discussed numerous ways to find God. The heart of his Christian realistic philosophy constitutes (idea of) a depth reason (immediate experience of (Proto)reality) and his philosophical (moral) psychology (Bartelj 1992; Žalec 2002, 9).

Milan Komar (Emilio Komar; 1921–2006), an important Slovene and Argentinean philosopher, deserves mention. In 1921 Komar was born in Ljubljana. He left Europe after the Second World War and he became a professor modern philosophy history at the Universidad Católica Argentina, where he lectured for decades. In 1992 he was honored by pope John Paul II. Komar in his realistic Christian philosophy was deeply inspired by the thought of Thomas Aquinas (Komar 2002). He dealt with the reperiodisation of philosophy, studied rationalistic traditions in detail, developed a critique of modern autonomous philosophy (Kant, Hegel, Marx, Adorno) and culture and made important contributions to depth psychology (Komar 1996).

Bojan Žalec (born 1966), a member of Juhant´s research group, researches Slovene philosophical tradition (he is the leading expert for F. Veber and his "school") (Žalec 2004, 241-263). Additionally, he engaged in detailed study regarding some phenomena of modern (19th and 20th century) philosophy. Žalec studies were interwoven with intentionality, semantic, and epistemological problems (Austrian philosophy, analytical philosophy), moral psychology, ethics (Ch. Taylor, A. MacIntyre, R. Rorty), and philosophical anthropology (Žalec 2002, 117-135).

Other philosophers are primarily engaged in the social and ideological questions of the society. Anton Stres published books on Marxist philosophy, social philosophy and ethics. Edi Kovač and Branko Klun along with Janez Juhant concentrate on the philosophy of post modernity (Klun 2000; Kovač 1994). The first two philosophers focus on Emmanuel Levinas. The philosophy of Martin Heidegger has been very influential in Slovenia. Robert Petkovšek presented Heidegger's relationship to Plato (Petkovšek 1998; Petkovšek 2004). Anton Jamnik worked on the issues of modern ethics. He discussed the main ideas of philosophers like Taylor and Rawls and evaluated their role in the (post)modern debate concerning basic ethical problems (Jamnik 1998). Vojko Strahovnik (2004, 2009), a very talented young philosopher is a member of the Faculty of Theology research group and the coordinator of international project *ETHOS – Ethical Education for a Sustainable and Dialogic Future*, which concentrates on the implementation of ethics for teachers and for educators in the kindergarten.

Štefan Ferenčak is involved with the Slovene Church music tradition. He wrote several theoretical discussions on this topic and published anthologies of Slovene Church music (Ferenčak 2002).

Jože Krašovec, Old Testament Professor and a member of the Slovenian Academy of Sciences and Arts wrote three dissertations: the first at the Pontifical Biblical Institute, the second at the Hebrew University in Jerusalem, and the third at the Sorbonne and Institut Catholique (Krašovec 1967, 1984, 1988). He has been elected President of the International Organization for the Study of the Old Testament (IOSOT). He was also responsible for organising the 19th IOSOT Congress in Ljubljana in July 2007. In 1984 he assumed responsibility for a new translation of the Bible into Slovene. This translation was intended to be an ecumenical version. The Bible translation was completed and published in the year 1996 as the Slovene Standard Version. Since 2001 he has been working systematically on Biblical names in the Original and in the European Bible translations (Krašovec 1999; 2000; 2001).

Terezija Snežna Večko translated the Books of Samuel, Ruth and Esther into the Slovene language. She focused her research on the meaning of guilt, punishment and forgiveness in the Books of Samuel and on repentant prayer in the time of the Second Temple (Večko 1995; 1998, 201-215). Since his dissertation in 1988 her colleague, Milan Matjaž, has been working on the synoptic tradition, especially on the Christological motifs of this tradition (Matjaž 1999; 2004, 269-284). His research further extends to the first Slovene translations of the Bible (Matjaž 2004, 357-366). The moral theologian, Anton Mlinar, works on the issues of biomedical ethics. He organized the translation of the Book by Bernard Häring *Frei sein in Christus*, and translated a portion of it into Slovene. Ivan Janez Štuhec concentrates on the social questions of the 20th century and on the relationship of the Church to these questions (Štuhec 1995; 2003).

The fundamental theologian, Drago Ocvirk, researches the relationship between modern culture and Christianity. He researches new institutional and symbolic forms of education, which will contribute to build the future European society. He is interested in the roles of religions, especially how they contribute to violence or the elimination of violence in modern societies. He examines as to how religious, institutional, symbolic elements and elements of teaching, which cause violence, could be discarded or respectively neutralized (Ocvirk 1998; 2000).

Because the Marxist ideologists are not prepared to discuss the problem of the communist past Church historians and independent philosophers experience many difficulties when opposing the Marxist doctrine in research and in the academic area. For former communists the revolution, in particular, is a taboo subject. The Church historians work diligently on clarifying the revolutionary period. They have edited the *Acta ecclesiastica Sloveniae* as important documents of the Church and Christianity's past. The editor, Bogdan Kolar, is a tenured professor in the field of Church History. He works on Slovenian emigration as a part of Slovenian national history and a challenge for Church communities both in the country of origin as well as in their new chosen country. He published a monograph treating the same topic (Kolar 2004). His second theme is the history of religious communities during the period of the totalitarian system in Slovenia and their history in general. A survey entitled "*The Impact of the Communist Period on the Life of Religious Communities*" has been already published as a section of a larger project.

Slavko Krajnc focuses on the inculturation of the liturgy in the Slovene tradition. He explores the importance of the Slovene liturgy, language and Church reformers such as bishop Tomaž Hren (1560–1630), parish-priest Franc Mihael Paglovec (1679–1759), the first Catholic translator of the Book of Tobias, bishop Karl Janez Herberstein (1717–1787), parish-priest Peter Pavel Glavar (1721–1784), bishop Anton Martin Slomšek (1800–1862) and ecclesiologist Franc Grivec (1878-1963). Krajnc encouraged Slovene priests and theologians to bring the liturgy closer to the people (Krajnc 2002; 2004).

Avguštin Lah devotes his studies to basic questions of human existence in connection to current challenges of the modern world. These are the questions of human person and society, as they arise from scientific developments and viewed from traditional religions. He tries to find answers to these questions in the light of biblical theological views on person and faith in God as a community of love (Lah 2004). He also examines questions from the Vatican Council (Lah 2000; 2003, 205-362).

Professor Anton Štrukelj was a member of the International Theological Commission selected by the Holy See. Currently he is the chief editor of the Slovene edition of the international Catholic bulletin, *Communio*. He worked on the theology of Hans Urs von Balthasar and on spiritual aspects of theology. As a visiting professor he lectured in Friebourg, Lugano and Sankt Petersburg (Štrukelj 2002; 2004).

Professor Ciril Sorč points out that the relationships in the Holy Trinity are the necessary conditions of relationships in human society. The Perichoresis can be an inspiration and hermeneutic principle for the relationships among people (Sorč 2005).

Stanko Gerjolj is a professor of Educational Psychology and Religious Education and an active member of the Juhant research group. His research is focused on the psychological processes of education, particularly in societies of the post-communist states. His work also includes diverse questions of psychology of religious education. Gerjolj's books for religious education (from 6th to 9th year of religious education) are based on the methods of Howard Gardners' theory of Multiple Intelligences and of Gestaltpedagogik, which supplement the traditional way of catechesis (Gerjolj 1997; 2000, 170-179; 2000, 44, 153-161; 2003, 133-137; 2004, 89-99).

Alojzij S. Snoj developed (with collaborators) a catechetical plan in Slovenia. It is the anthropological-kerygmatical model of reciprocity. The Slovene catechisms were written based upon this model (Snoj 2000, 2003).

In her research and numerous publications Erika Prijatelj has focused on the connections among theology, developmental psychology and education. In 2010 she was awarded an international scholarship by ETE (Ecumenical Theological Education) and two years later she completed her post-doctoral work in pastoral studies at CTU (Catholic Theological Union), Chicago, IL, USA. Since 2012 she has been a scholar at Boston College, Chestnut Hill, MA, USA.

Peter Kvaternik is a member of several international associations of pastoral theologians. Together with Juhant, Potočnik and Valenčič he guided the research project "Rapture". They researched the changes in the ten former communist countries as compared with the other totalitarian systems of the 20th century. The pastoral-theologian work of Kvaternik is dedicated to the challenges regarding the Church's message of good news to the (post)modern world (Kvaternik 2001; 2004).

Christian Gostečnik (2012; 2013) has developed a master's program as well as a program for family therapy specialists. It is a highly acclaimed therapeutic program for families. He has published several books on these topics.

Theology and freedom

We have already discussed the topic regarding the freedom of theology. This is a very important issue, especially in the former communist countries. To combine the concepts "belief" and "knowing" is to make a square circle. The impossibility to know the "last" truth of man and the world leads us to the mystery (Rahner 1961, 56) of faith and to the *theologia negativa.* As Rahner pointed out: "The history of the concept of theology has in its foundation the conflict between poetic-religious grounding in mythology and conceptual-philosophical grounding in metaphysics." (Bayer, Peters 1998, 1081) He has in his mind the Antic background, but the issue still remains and it is related to the problem of freedom of theological investigation. The Slovene theological authors pointed out this problem in different ways. They are more or less dependent on the past with the pressure of the communist regime. They deal with the question of freedom in the area of: philosophical streams, ideology and transition, societal dimension of the human rights, religion and violence, person for the ethical challenge of science and especially for the economical processes of globalisation, questions of didactic and pastoral in the transition, the problems of post-modern society and the possibilities for the theology and the Church in the individualized society. They research different forms of fundamentalism, the relationships between religion and violence, and the role of the scripture and the Catholic tradition in these processes in the Church and in the society. The relationship between the Church (theology) and society is a very important one, because individualism in present in society and in the Church.

Above all, the question of freedom should not be excluded or marginalized in the Church (Juhant 2005). The question of freedom (in God) could only be solved – through the perspective of Rahner and

Schnackenburg - in the willingness for a permanent hearing to the history of the relationship between human person and God, and also based upon the existential experience. This means an openness for reciprocal hearing and speaking in the community of the Church.

The role of theology is more and more difficult. On one hand theology is less frequently questioned by society and in particular by individual persons. People are ready to solve their problems by themselves; they no longer desire to submit to Church hierarchical statements and directives. Despite self-isolation, the postmodern person is not willing to submit to a community and, in particular, this person is not willing to submit to an organized group or institution like the Church. On the other hand the postmodern person suffers because of self-isolation.

Finding one's new role in the world today is extremely difficult for everyone but much more difficult for the post-communist man/woman.

Theology has a very thankless task in attempting to show the way of freedom to the individualized man/woman. However, this task is also thankless from another point of view. The institutional Church is neither ready nor able to accept the situation of the postmodern person. The attitude of the postmodern person frightens the Church. Because of this the Church, as an institution, strives to limit the movement toward freedom with the intention to save the postmodern man/woman from the perils of an individualised life. Despite this theologians are challenged to deal with human freedom and they need to maintain this tension between the individual freedom of the modern person and the freedom of the children of God. The institutional Church is required to support this balance. Whether the Church can survive these opposing energies is today's burning question. The postmodern man/woman and society would be the beneficiaries of a successful resolution. However, it is an enormous challenge to change the Church and as Beck pointed out: The Church is an important institution of globalization, which has all the structures of globalisation, but it has to be willing to change if it wants to overcome its present zombielike state. This is not only a problem of the Church in Slovenia, but also a problem of the entire Catholic Church in the postmodern world (Beck 2000, 279).

REFERENCES

Acta Synodalia sacrosancti Concilii Oecumenici Vaticani II, vol. III, 804-805. 1977. Congregationes Generales CXXXIII-CXXXVII. Città del Vaticano: Typ. Polygl. Vat.

Allport, Gordon W. 1968. The Historical Background of Modern Social Psychology. In: Gardner Lindzey, ed. *The Handbook of Social Psychology*, Vol 1, 1-80. New York: Random House.

Anders, Güther. 1992. *Die Antiquiertheit des Menschen I, II*. München: Beck.

Anders, Güther. 1996. *Ketzereien*. München: Beck.

Annas, Julia. 1994. *Introduction à la République de Platon*. Paris: P.U. F.

Akvinski, Tomaž. 1999. *Izbrani filozofski spisi* [*Selected Philosophical Works*]. Ljubljana: Družina.

Aquinas, Thomas. 1961. *Summae Theologiae* (STh) (5 volumes). Madrid: La Editorial Catholica.

Arendt, Hannah. 1979. *The Origins of Totalitarianism*. Harcourt: Harcourt Brace Jovanovich.

Arendt, Hannah. 2005. *Izvori totalitarizma* [*The Origins of Totalitarianism*]. Ljubljana: Claritas.

Aristoteles. 1995. *Philosophsiche Schriften. 3 (Ethics) and 5 (Metaphysics)*. Hamburg: Meiner.

Aristoteles. 1999. *Metafizika* [*Metaphysics*]. Ljubljana: ZRC.

Augustin. 1975. De Trinitate. 15, 1,1. In: *Patres Latini*. Tom. 42. Turnoholti: Migne.

Avsenik Nabergoj, *Irena. 2013. Reality and Truth in Literature. From Ancient to Modern European Literary and Critical Discourse.* Goettingen: V&R Unipress.

Barnett, Lincoln. 1950. *Einstein und das Universum*. Frankfurt/ Amsterdam: Bermann-Fischer/Querido Verlag.

Bartelj, Ludvik. 1970. *Človek-svet-Bog* [*Man-World-God*]. Ljubljana: private ed.

Bartelj, Ludvik. 1983. *Globinski razum in Prastvarnost I-II* [Depth Reason and Protoreality]. Ljubljana/Maribor: private ed. /Večer.

Bartelj, Ludvik. 1992. *Globinska psihologija religije* [*Depth Psychology of Religion* (in two volumes)]. Ljubljana: private ed.

Baudrillard, Jean. 2010. *The Agony of Power*. Los Angeles: Semiotext(e).

Bauer, Joachim. 2006. *Prinzip Menschlichkeit*. Hamburg: Hoffmann und Campe.

Bauman, Zygmunt. 1996. *Dialektik der Ordnung. Die Moderne und Holocaust*. Hamburg: Europäische Verlagsanstalt/Sabine Groenewold Verlage.

Bauman, Zygmund. 2002. *Dialektik der Ordnung* [*Dialectic of the Order*]. Hamburg: Europäische Verlagsanstalt.

Bauman, Zygmunt. 1993. *Postmodern Ethics*. Cambridge: Politiy Press.

Bauman, Zygmunt.1995. *Postmoderne Ethik*. Hamburg: Hamburger Edition.

Bauman, Zygmunt. 1991. *Modernity and Ambivalence*. Cambridge: Politiy Press.

Bauman, Zygmunt.1998. *Globalisation: the Human Consequences*. Cambridge: Polity Press.

Bayer, Oswald, and Albrecht Peters. 1998. Theologie. In: Joachim Ritter and Karlfried Gründer. *Hist. Wört. der Philosophie,* Bd. X, 1081. Basel: Schwabe AG.

Beck, Ulrich. 1996. *Risikogesellschaft. Auf dem Weg in eine andere Moderne*. Frankfurt: Suhrkamp.

Beck, Ulrich. 2000. *Freiheit oder Kapitalismus, Gesellschaft zu denken*. Frankfurt: Suhrkamp.

Beck, Ulrich, Juhant, Janez and Žalec, Bojan (eds.). 2010. *Art of life: origins, foundations and perspectives*, (Theologie Ost-West, Bd. 14). Wien; Zürich; Berlin: LIT.

Benedict XVI. 2009. *Caritas in Veritate*. Cerkveni dokumenti 127. Ljubljana: Družina.

Berdjajew, Nikolai.1977. *Wahrheit und Lüge des Kommunismus*. Wien: Neue Mitte.

Berlin, Isaiah. 1997. *The Proper Study of Mankind*. London: Chatto&Windus.

Biel, Robert. 1996. *Lebens - und Todeszeichen der Kirche in Polen*. Innsbruck.

Bin Laden, Osama. 1998. Interview. http://www.pbs.org/wgbh/pages/frontline/shows/binladen/who/interview.html; accessed 20.4.2002.

Biser, Eugen.1995. *Der Mensch – das uneingelöste Versprechen. Entwurf einer Modalanthropologie*. Düsseldorf: Pathmos.

Böckenförde, E. Wolfgang. 1976. *Staat, Gesellschaft, Freiheit. Studien zur Staatstheorie und zum Verfassungsrecht*. Frankfurt am Main: Suhrkamp.Boethius, Anicius Manlius Torquatus Severinus. 1999. Trs. Matjaž Vesel. *Opuscula sacra. Filozofsko teološki traktati*. Ljubljana: ZRC.

Boff, Leonardo. 2011. *Sehnsucht nach dem Unendlichen. Spirituell Leben*. Kevelaer: Butzon&Bercker.

Brague, Rémi. 1998. Le problème de l'homme moderne. In: Guy Laforest and Philippe de Lara, eds. *Charles Taylor et l'interprétation de l'identité moderne*. Paris: Cerf.

Bürger, Peter. 2000. *Ursprung des posmodernen Denkens*. Weilerswist: Velbrück GmbH.

Cacho, Lydia. 2011. *Sklaverei: Im Inneren des Milliardengeschäfts Menschenhandel*. Frankfurt: S. Fischer.

Cassirer, Ernst. 1974/1944. *An Essay on Man*. Princeton: Yale University Press.

Cavanaugh, William T. 2009. *The Myth of Religious Violence. Secular Ideology and the Roots of Modern Conflict*. Oxford: UP.

Cavanaugh, William T. 2010. *Theopolitical Investigation*. New York: T&T Clar k.

Chomsky, Noam. 2004. Lecture at University of Manchester. Department of Government 22 May 2004. Sounded Out Films (DVD) (by Skrimshire 2008, 1).

Cicero. 1975. *De oficiis 1*. Cambridge, Mass: Harvard University Press.

Convention on the Prevention and Punishment of the Crime of Genocide. 1948.http://web.archive.org/web/20080502140534/http://www.unhchr.ch/html/menu3/b/p_genoci.htm; accessed on 1.8. 2013.

Coreth, Emerich, Walter M. Neidl, and Georg Pfligersdorffer. 1987. *Christliche Philosophie im katholischen Denken des 19. und 20. Jahrhunderts*. Vol. I, II. Graz/Wien/Köln: Styria Premium.

Cournand, André. 1977. The Code of the Scientist and its Relationship to Ethics. *Science* 198: 699-705.

Dalai Lama. 2004. *Ethics for the New Millennium*. Redword City, CA: The Dalaj Lama Fundation.

Darwin, Charles. 1859. *On the Origin of Species by Means of Natural Selection or the Perservation of Favoured Races in the Struggle for Life*. London: John Murray.

Dawkins, Richard. 1999. *The Selfish Gene*. Oxford/New York: Oxford University Press.

De Mause, Lloyd. 2005. *Das Emotionale Leben der Nationen*. Klagenfurt: Drava.

Denzinger, Henricus, and Adolfus Schönmetzer (DS). 1965. *Enchiridion symbolorum definitionum et Declarationum der rebus fidei et morum*. Barcinone: Herder.

Dumouchel, Paul, and Jean-Pierre Dupuy. 1999. *Die Hölle der Dinge. René Girard und die Logik der Ökonomie*. Thaur/Münster: Druck und Verlagshaus MbH/LIT.

Durkheim, Emil. 1992. *Samomor. Prepoved incesta in njeni izviri*. (*Suicide. Prohibition of Incest and its Origins*) Ljubljana: Filoz. knjižnica Škuc, Studia humanitatis.

Eder, Rebecca A. and Sarah C. Mangelsdorf. 1997. The Emotional Basis of Early Personality Developement. Implications for the Emergent Self-Concept. In: Robert Hogan, John Johnson and Stephen Brings, eds. *Handbook of Personality Psychology*, 209-240. San Diego: Academic Press.

Ehrlich, Lambert.1936a. Ruski boljševizem (Russian Bolshevism). In: *ČAS* XVIII (1923/24), 192-217, 275-295.

Ehrlich, Lambert. 1936b. Boljševizem v Kini (Bolshevism in China). In: *Misijonski koledar* XVIII (1936), 97-99.

Feiner, Johannes. 1965. *Offenbarung und Kirche-Kirche und Offenbarung*. In: Johannes Feiner and Magnus Löhrer. *Mysterium salutis* I, 497-544. Einsiedeln usw.: Benziger.

Ferenčak, Štefan. 2002. Kirchenlied und nationale Identität in Slowenien [Hymnody and National Identity in Slovenia]. In: *Internationale Arbeitsgemeinschaft für Hymnologie*. Bulletin 28. (Rijksuniversiteit Groningen: Instituut voor Liturgiewetenschap - About the polyphonic identity of Slovene national and artificial songs).

Ferenčak, Štefan. 2002. *Lepa si lepa si, roža Marija (Beautiful You are, rose Maria). Ein Beispiel historischer Volksmusikforschung*. Asco art & science Bratislava.

Ferenčak, Štefan. 2004. *Izobraževanje cerkvenih glasbenikov v mariborski škofiji od A. M. Slomška do danes 1836-2004*. [*The Education of the Churcsh Musicians in the Dioceses Maribor from A. M. Slomšek until today: 1836-2004*]. Maribor: Slomškova založba.

Fichte, Johann Gottlieb. 1965. Erste Einleitung in die Wissenschaftslehre. In: Immanuel Hermann Fichte, ed. *Sämtliche Werke I*. Berlin: Walter de Gruyter.

Flanagan, Owen. 1991. *Varieties of Moral Personality*. Cambridge, Mass.: Harvard University Press.

Flasch, Kurt. 2000. *Das philosophische Denken im Mittelalter*. Stuttgart: Reclam.

Foucault, Michel. 1980. *Powers and Strategies*. In: Colin Gordon(ed.), (trns. Colin Gordon and others), London: Harvester Press.

Fromm, Erich. 2007. *To Have or to Be*. New York: Continuum books (1976).

Fuchs, Ottmar. 2007. Wenn Wissen die Weisheit verhindert. Die (post)moderne Wissensgesellschaft als akute Herausforderung für christliches Glauben und Handeln. In: Janez Juhant and Bojan Žalec, eds. *On Cultivating Faith and Science: Reflections on Two Key Topics of Modern Ethics*, 157-172. Münster: LIT.

Fukuyama, Francis. 2000. *The Great Disruption: Human Nature and the Reconstitution of Social Order*. New York: Touchstone.

Gadamer, Hans-Georg. 1993. *Wahrheit und Methode, Gesammelte Werke 2, Hermeneutik* II. Tübingen: J. C. B Mohr.

Gaiser, Laris. 2007. Država na papirju [The State on Paper]. *Mag.* Ljubljana, 7. February 2007.

Gandhi, M.K. 1987. *An Autobiography or The Story of My Experiments with Truth.* Harmondsworth: Penguin Books.

Garaudy, Roger, John Baptist Metz, and Karl Rahner. 1970. *Der Dialog.* Reinbeck b. Hamburg.

Gelhaus, Petra. 2006. *Gentherapie und Welt-anschauung. Ein Überblick über die genethische Disskussion.* Darmstadt: Wissenschaftliche Buchgesellschaft.

Gergen, Keneth J. 1991. *The Saturated Self.* New York: Basic Books.

Gergen, Kenneth J. 1996. *Das Übersätigte Selbst.* Heidelberg: Carl Auer Systeme Verlag.

Gerjolj, Stanko. 1997. *Ideologie und Bildung: ideologisch-politischer Totalitarismus im Bildungs- und Erziehungswesen im Kommunismus und der Versuch einer Demokratisierung am Beispiel Sloweniens.* Texte zum Ost-West-Dialog, 12. Gießen: Justus-Liebig-Universität.

Gerjolj, Stanko. 2000. Beziehungen zwischen den Generationen: in einer sich vom Totalitarismus zur Demokratie bewegenden Gesellschaft. *Religionspädagogische Beiträge*, 44, 153-161.

Gerjolj, Stanko. 2000. Herausforderungen für eine Erziehung ohne Feindbilder. In: Czirják, J., ed. *Der Wille zu den Werten*, 170-179. Kaposvar: Szerzők.

Gerjolj, Stanko. 2003. Kommunikative Theologie und die Frage der multiplen Intelligenz. Workshop – Kommunikative Theologie im Vollzug. In: Hilbareth, B. J., Kraml, M., Scharer, M., eds. *Wahrheit in Beziehung*, 133-137. Mainz.

Gerjolj, Stanko. 2004. Vzgoja in izobraževanje pred nekaterimi izzivi globalizacije. [Education and Formation and some challenges of Globalization]. In: Ministrstvo za šolstvo in šport. *Kakšna bo šola prihodnosti*? 89-99, Ljubljana: Didakta.

Gerjolj, Stanko. 2006. *Živeti, delati, ljubiti* [*Living, Working and Loving*]. Celje: Mohorjeva družba.

Gilson, Étienne. 1984. *From Aristotle to Darwin and Back again.* Notre Dame: University Press.

Girard, René. 1972. *La violence et le sacré*. Paris: Grasset.

Girard, René. 1979. *Violence and the Sacred*. Baltimore: John Hopkins UP.

Girard, René. 1987. *Things Hidden since the Foundation of the World*. Standford: University Press.

Girard, René. 1989. *The Scapegoat*. Baltimore: John Hopkins UP.

Girard, René. 1997. *Wenn all das beginnt … Dialog mit Michael Treguer Aus dem Französischen von Pascal Veldboer,* 29. Thaur/Münster: LIT.

Girard, René. 1999. *Je vois Satan tomber comme l'éclair*. Paris: Grasset.

Girard, René. 2000. *Mimesis & Theory*. Stanford: UP.

Girard, René. 2001. *I See Satan Fall Like Lightning*. Maryknoll: Orbis Books.

Gostečnik, Christian. 2012. *Govorica telesa v psihoanalizi* [*The Body Language in Psychoanalysis*]. Ljubljana: Brat Frančišek/ Teološka fakulteta: Frančiškanski družinski inštitut.

Gostečnik, Christian. 2013. *Relacijska paradigma in klinična praksa psihoanalizi* [*Relational Paradigm and Clinical Practice*]. Ljubljana: Brat Frančišek: Frančiškanski družinski institut.

Grinnell, Frederick. 1992. *The Scientific Attitude*. New York/London: Guilford Press.

Grivec, Franc. 1960. *Konstantin und Method, Lehrer der Slawen*. Wiesbaden: Otto Harrassowitz.

Guisep, Nay. 2004. Die Kirche und die Menschenrechte, als Rechte auch des Menshen als Geschöpf Gottes. In: *Bulletin. ET 15*. Jg. Heft 2, 289f.

Guitton, Jean. 1970. *Histoire et destinée*. Paris: Cerf.

Guitton, Jean. 1992. *Što verujem*. Zagreb: KS.

Haas, Alois M. 2007. *Mystik als Aussage. Erfahrungs- Denk- und Redeformen christlcihen Mystik*. Frankfurt/Leipzig: Verlag der Weltreligionen.

Habermas, Jürgen. 2001. *Zeit der Übergänge*. Frankfurt: Suhrkamp.

Habermas, Jürgen. 2005. *Glauben und Wissen*. Frankfurt: Suhrkamp.

Hack, Susan. 1995. *Evidence and Inquiry: Towards Reconstruction in Epistemology*. Oxford: Blackwell.

Hagan, Frank E. 1997. *Political Crime: Ideology and Criminality*. Boston: Allyn and Bacon.

Havel, Vaclav. 2012. Hoffnung. V: Limbeck, Meinrad. *Abschied vom Opfertod. Das Christentum neu denken.* Ostfildern: Mathias Grünewald (Schwaben), 11-11.

Hegel, Georg Wilhelm Friedrich. 1975 (1807). *Philosophie des Geistes*. Frankfurt: Suhrkamp.

Heidegger, Martin. 1967. *Existence and Being*. Werner Brock, Introduction and Analysis. Chicago: Gateway.

Hobsbawm, Eric. 1996. *The Age of Revolution: Europe 1789-1848*. New York: Vintage Books (first published 1962. London: Weidenfeld & Nickolson).

Hollis, Martin. 1994. *The Philosophy of Social Science. An Introduction*. Cambridge: University Press.

Horster, Detlef. 1999. *Postchristliche Moral. Eine sozialphilosophische Begründung*. Hamburg: Junius.

Hünermann, Peter, Juhant, Janez and Žalec, Bojan (eds.). 2007. *Dialogue and Virtue: Ways to Overcome Clashes of our Civilizations*, (Theologie Ost-West, Bd. 10). Münster: LIT.

Huntington, Samuel P. 1993. *The Clash of Civilizations*. New York: Foreign Affairs.

Huysteen van, J. Wentzel. 2006. *Alone in the World? Human Uniqueness in Science and Theo*logy. Göttingen: Vandenhoeck&Ruprecht

Immel, Karl Albrecht and Tränkle, Klaus. 2011. *Aktenzeichen Armut. Globalisierung in Texten und Grafiken*. Wuppertal: Peter Hammer Verlag.

James, William. 2002. *The Varieties of Religious Experience. A Study in the Human Nature*. London and New York: Routledge

Jamnik, Anton, 1998. *Liberalizem in vprašanje etike* [*Liberalism and the Question of Ethics*]. Ljubljana: Nova revija.

Janžekovič, Janez. 1978. Dušno pastirstvo v skladu z današanjim družbenim razvojem [The Soulcare in Acordance with the Current Development]. In: *Izbrani spisi* [*Selected Works*], 148. Celje. I.

Jaspers, Karl. 1951. *Über die Bedigungen und Möglichkeiten des neuen Humanismus*. Frankfurt: Suhrkamp.

Jaspers, Karl. 1962. *Der philosophische Glaube angesichts der christlichen Offenbarung*. München: Piper.

Jonas, Hans. 1979. *Prinzip der Verantwortung*. Frankfurt: Suhrkamp.

Jonas, Hans. 1987. *Der Gottesbegriff nach Auschwitz: eine jüdische Stimme*. Frankfurt: Suhrkamp.

Judt, Tony and Timothy Snyder. 2012. *Thinking Twentieth Century*. New York: Pinguin.

Juhant, Janez, and Stanko Janežič. 1998. *Janez Evangelist Krek*. Maribor: Slomškova založba.

Juhant, Janez, and Vinko Potočnik, eds. 2002. *Mislec in kolesja ideologij: Filozof Janez Janžekovič*. [*The Thinker and the Wheels of Ideology: Philosopher Janez Janžekovič*] Ljubljana: Družina.

Juhant, Janez, ed. 2000. *Kaj pomeni religija za človeka. Znanstvena podoba religije* [*The Significance of Religion for Man. The Scientific Image of Religion*]. Ljubljana: Družina/TEOF.

Juhant, Janez. 1978. *Entschiedenheit über die Wirklichkeit. Transzendental-ontologische Voraussetzungen des Denkens von Georg Hermes*. Innsbruck (Diss.Mas.).

Juhant, Janez. 1997. *Na poti k resnici in spravi* [*On the Way to Truth and Reconciliation*]. Ljubljana: TEOF.

Juhant, Janez. 2000. Antropološki problemi študija religije danes [Anthropological Problems of the Study of Religion Today]. In: Janez Juhant, ed. *Kaj pomeni religija za človeka. Znanstvena podoba religije* [*What Does Religion Mean for the Man. Scientific Image of Religion*]. Ljubljana: Družina/ZRC TEF.

Juhant, Janez. 2000. *Teologija na prelomu časov* [*Theology at the Break of Times*]. Ljubljana: TEOF/Družina.

Juhant, Janez. 2001. *Zgodovina filozofije* [*History of Philosophy. Antiquity and the Middle Ages*]. Ljubljana: Družina.

Juhant, Janez. 2003. *Človek v iskanju svoje podobe.Filozofska antropologija.* [*Man Searching for his Image. Philosophical Anthropology*]. Ljubljana: Claritas.

Juhant, Janez. 2003. *Etika ali človeškost. Filozofski temelji etike* [*Ethics or Humanity. Philosophical Foundations of Ethics*]. Ljubljana: Teološka fakulteta.

Juhant, Janez. 2005. *Globalisierung, Kirche und post moderner Mensch.* Münster: LIT.

Juhant, Janez. 2006. Autonomous person as the basis of ethics: man between modern and postmodern morality. In: Janez Juhant and Bojan Žalec, eds. *Person and Good: Man and his Ethics in the Postmodern World*. Theologie Ost-West, Bd 6. Münster: LIT.

Juhant, Janez and Bojan Žalec (eds.). 2007. *On Cultivating Faith and Science : Reflections on two Key Topics of Modern Ethics*, (Theologie Ost-West, Bd. 9). Münster: LIT.

Juhant, Janez and Bojan Žalec (eds.). 2008. *Surviving Globalization: the Uneasy Gift of Interdependence*, (Theologie Ost-West, Europäische Perspektiven, Bd. 13). Berlin: LIT.

Juhant, Janez. 2008. *Im Feuer der europäischen Ideenzüge : Slowenien*, (Europa 2020, Bd. 24). Wien; Zürich; Berlin; Münster: LIT.

Juhant, Janez and Bojan Žalec (eds.). 2011. *Humanity after Selfish Prometheus: Chances of Dialogue and Ethics in a Technicized World*, (Theologie Ost-West, Bd. 15). Münster: LIT.

Juhant, Janez and Bojan Žalec (eds.). 2012. *Reconciliation : the Way of Healing and Growth*, (Theologie Ost-West, Bd. 16). Zürich; Münster: LIT.

Kamlah, Wilhelm. 1973. *Philosophische Anthropologie.* Mannheim: B.I. Hochschultaschenbücher.

Kant, Immanuel. 1956/1788. *Kritik der praktischen Vernunft.* In: Wilhelm Weischedel (ed.). *Werke in zwölf Bänden.*VII. Frankfurt/Wiesbaden: Suhrkamp/Insel. (Riga: J-F.- Hartknoch), 107-302.

Kant, Immanuel. 1956. *Kritik der reinen Vernunft.* In: Wilhelm Weischedel (ed.). *Werke in zwölf Bänden.* III/IV. Frankfurt/Wiesbaden: Suhrkamp/Insel.

Kant, Immanuel. 1958. *Logik*. Königsberg 1800, A 25. In: Wilhelm Weischedel (ed.) *Werke in zwölf Bänden. VI*, 447-449. Frankfurt/Wiesbaden: Suhrkamp/Insel.

Kant, Immanuel. 1964. Beantwortung der Frage: Was ist die Aufklärung? In: Wilhelm Weischedel (ed.) *Kant, Werke in zwölf Bänden* XI. Frankfurt/Wiesbaden: Suhrkamp/Insel, 53-61.

Kast, Verena. 2003. *Trotz allem Ich*. Freiburg/Basel/Wien: Herder.

Kertész, Imre. 2003. *Liquidation*. Frankfurt: Suhrkamp.

Kiepas, Andrzej. 2010. *Der Mensch. Das vergessene Paradigma der Technikphilosophie*? Berlin: LIT.

Klun, Branko. 2000. *Das Gute vor dem Sein. Levinas versus Heidegger*. Frankfurt am Main et al: Peter Lang.

Knapp, Marcus. 2006. *Verantwortetes Christsein heute. Theologie zwischen Metaphysik und Postmoderne*. Freiburg/Basel/Wien: Herder.

Kolar, Bogdan. 2004. *Slovenian Priests and Priests of Slovenian Descent in the Catholic Communities of California*. San Francisco: Educational and Dramatic Club Slovenia.

Komar, Emilio. 1996. *Orden y Misterio*. Buenos Aires: Fraternitas/Emecé.

Komarica, Franjo. 2001. *U obrani obespravljenih* [*In the Defense of the Rightless*]. Banja Luka: Bishop's Ordinary of Banja Luka/Zagreb: Croatian Heritage Foundation.

Kovač, Edvard. 1994. Le face-à-face. In: *Le visage*. Autrement, N. 148, Octobre.

Krajnc, Slavko. 2002. L'attiva partecipazione liturgica nella Chiesa Slovena come preparazione al Concilio Vaticano II. In: Domenico Sartore, Agostino Montan and Manlio Sodi, eds. *Actuosa participatio: conoscere, comprendere e vivere la liturgia: studi in onore del Domenico Sartore*, (*Monumenta studia instrumenta liturgica*, 18). Citta del Vaticano: Editrice Vaticana.

Krajnc, Slavko. 2004. Il rito della purificazione e della benedizione della puerpera con l'esempio dell'inculturazione slovena. In: *Bogoslovni vestnik*, v. 64, n. 4. pp. 663-676.

Kraml, Hans. 1984. *Die Rede von Gott sprachkritisch rekonstruiert aus Sentenzenkommentaren*. Innsbruck: Tyrolia.

Krašovec, Jože. 1967. *Der Merismus im Biblisch-Hebraeischen und Nordwestsemitischen*. Roma: Pontifical Biblical Institue.

Krašovec, Jože. 1984. *Antithetic Structure in Biblical Hebrew Poetry*. Leiden: E. J. Brill.

Krašovec, Jože. 1988. *La Justice (sdq) de Dieu dans la Bible hébraïque et l'interprétation juive et chrétienne*. Freiburg/Göttingen: Universitätsverlag/Vandenhoeck & Ruprecht.

Krašovec, Jože. 1999. *Reward, Punishment, and Forgiveness*. Leiden/Ljubljana: Brill Academic Publishers/Slovenian Academy of Sciences and Arts.

Krašovec, Jože. 2000. *Between Guilt and Reconciliation*. Ljubljana: Slovenian Academy of Sciences and Arts.

Krašovec, Jože. 2001. *Between Original and Translations*. Ljubljana: Slovenian Academy of Sciences and Arts.

Küng, Hans. 1990. *Project Weltethos*. München: Piper.

Küng, Hans. 2007. *Islam. Past, Present and Future*. Oxford: Oneworld.

Kurz, Robert. 2003. *Weltordnungskrieg*. Bad Honnef: Horlemann.

Kuschel, Karl Josef. 2008. Sterben in Gott hinein. *Publik-Forum,* 22. February. Nr. 4, 52-56.

Kvaternik, Peter. 2001. Stalno pod naponom: obiteljski pastoral pred izazovom slobodnoga vremena [The Pastoral of Family under the Challenge of Freetime]. *Diacovensia*, 9(1), 169-188, Đakovo, HR.

Kvaternik, Peter. 2004. *Im Herzen Europas: Kirche und Gesellschaft in Slowenien*. Diakonia Jg. 35, Nr. 4. Mainz, 1972), Jul. 2004.

Kvaternik, Peter. 2004. *Seelsorgekonzepte im Wiederzusammenhang*. Pastor.theol. Inf., 2003, Jg. 23, Heft 1, Schwerte, DE.

Lah, Avguštin. 1964. *Družina* 13, 161, 1. October.

Lah, Avguštin. 1964. Odločilno važni dnevi koncila [The Decisive Days of the Council]. In: *Koncilska priloga "Družine"* [*Council Supplement of "Družina"*] 13, 185 - 192, 15. October.

Lah, Avguštin. 1964. Zgodovinski dan v življenju Cerkve [The Historical Day in the Life of Church]. In: *Družina* 13, 246-247, 15. December.

Lah, Avguštin. 2000. *Bog Oče. Skrivnost božje bližine* [*God-Father. The Secret of the Nearness of God*]. Ljubljana: Družina.

Lah, Avguštin. 2001. Sprejem 2. Vatikanskega koncila v Sloveniji [The Reception of the Second Vatican Council in Slovenia]. In: Peter Kvaternik. *V prelomnih časih* [*In the Times of Rapture*], 9-31. Ljubljana: Družina.

Lah, Avguštin. 2003. Teološka antropologija. In: Ciril Sorč, ed. *Priročnik dogmatične teologije I* [*Enchiridion of the Dogmatical Theology*], 205-362. Ljubljana: Družina.

Lah, Avguštin. 2004. Globalisierungsängste und christliches Gott- und Menschenverständnis. In: Adrian Loretan, Franco Luzatto, eds. *Gesellschaftliche Ängste als theologische Herausforderung*. Kontext Europa, (Theologie Ost - West, Tome 3), 171-182, Münster: LIT.

Lah, Avguštin. 2004. Podobe Boga sodnika med nasiljem in nenasiljem [Images of God the Judge between Violence and Non-Violence]. In: *Bogoslovni vestnik,* V. 64, Nr. 4, 601-616.

Lajovic, Dušan. 2001. *Med svobodo in rdečo zvezdo* [*Between the Freedom and the Red Star*]. Ljubljana: Nova obzorja.

Lavrič, Miran, in Sergej Flere. 2007. Razlage religije z vidika sodobnih teorij evolucijske psihologije. In: *Anthropos*, 39, Nr. 3-4, 11-21.

Levinas, Emmanuel. 1987. *Totalität und Unendlichkeit.* Versuch über die Exteriorität. Freiburg/München: Karl Alber.

Lezzi-Hafter, Adienne. 2000. Oidipus. In: Hubert Cancik and Helmuth Schneider, eds. *Der Neue Pauly. Enzyklopädie der Antike,* 1130-1133. Stuttgart: J.B.Metzler.

Lippmann, Walter. 1955. *Essays in the Public Philosophy*. Boston: Little Brown.

Löw, Konrad. 1999. *Das Rotbuch der kommunistischen Ideologie.* München: Langen Müller.

MacIntyre, Alasdair. 1986. *After Virtue*. Notre Dame: University Press.

MacIntyre, Alasdair. 1999. *Dependent Rational Animals. Why Human Beings Need the Virtues*. London: Duckworth.

Macintyre, Alasdair. 2001. *Die Anerkennung der Abhängigkeit. Über menschliche Tugenden*. Hamburg: Rotbuch Relationen.

MacIntyre, Alasdair. 2003 /1991. *Three Rival Versions of Moral Enquiry. Encyclopedia. Genealogy and Tradition*. Notre Dame: University Press.

Marten, Rainer. 2000. *Menschliche Wahrheit*. München: Fink.

Máté-Toth, András. 2001. Konzilsrezeption. In: András Máté-Tóth and Pavel Miklušcák. *Kirche im Aufbruch*, 344. Ostfildern: Schwabenverlag.

Matjaž, Maksimilijan. 1999. *Furcht und Gotteserfahrung: die Bedeutung des Furchtmotivs für die Christologie des Markus*. Forschung zur Bibel, Bd. 91. Würzburg: Echter.

Matjaž, Maksimilijan. 2004. The Fear on the Way to Jerusalem: the Overlooking Sight of the Christological Concept in the Gospel of Mark. In: Artur Malina, ed. *On his Way: Studies in Honour of Professor Klemens Stock, on the Occasion of his 70th Birthday*, 269-284. Katowice: Księgarnia św. Jacka.

Matjaž, Maksimilijan.2004. Prevajanje Svetega pisma v času škofa Herbersteina [The Translation of the Bible in the Time of Bishop Herberstein]. In: Edo Škulj, ed. *Herbersteinov simpozij v Rimu* [*Herberstein's Symposium in Rome*], 357-366, Celje: Mohorjeva družba.

McAllister, Ted V. 1997. *Revolt Against Modernity*. Kansas: University Press.

McInerny, Ralph. 1995. Ethics. In: Norman Kretzmann and Eleonore Stump, eds. *The Cambridge Companion to Aquinas*. Cambridge: University Press.

McLuhan, Marshall. 1967. *The Medium is the Message. An Inventory of Effects*. New York: Ginkho.

McLuhan, Marshall. 1989. *The Global Village*. Oxford: University Press.

Merkel, Reinhard. 2002. Verbrauchende Embrionenforschung? In: Reinold Schmücker and Ulrich Steinvorth. *Gerechtigkeit und Politik: Philosophische Perspektiven*. Berlin: Akademie Verlag.

Milčinski, Lev. 1986. *Samomor in Slovenci* [*Suicide and Slovenes*]. Ljubljana: CZ.

Mieth, Dietmar. 2007. *Meister Eckhart Jahrbuch,* 71-96. Vol.1. Stuttgart: Kohlhammer Verlag.

Milgram, Stanley. 1974. *Obedience to Authority: En Experimental View*. London: Tavistock Publications.

Muck, Otto. 1999. *Rationalität und Weltanschaung*. Innsbruck/Wien: Tyrolia.

Müller, Edda. 2010: acc. 03 August 2010: http://www.transparency.org/news_room/latest_news/press_releases_nc/2010/2010_06_20_germany_board.

Murphy, Jeffrie G. 2009. The Unhappy Immoralist. In: Steven M. Cahn, ed. *Exploring Ethics,* 64-67. New York: Oxford University Press.

Murphy, Mark C. (ed.). 2003. *Alasdair MacIntyre*. Cambridge: University Press.

Nadškofija-archives. 1942. *Poročilo z dekanijske konference v Novem mestu* [*Report of the Dean-Conference of Novo Mesto*]. Ljubljana: F 37.

Nietzsche, Friedrich. 1988. *Onstran dobrega in zlega. H genealogiji morale* [*Beyond Good* and *Evil*, *On the Genealogy Of Morality*]. Ljubljana: SM.

Novalis. 1963. Monolog. Die Lerhlinge zu Sais. Die Christenheit oder Europa. Hymnen an die Nacht. Geistliche Lieder. Heinrich von Ofterdingen. Reinbeck. In: Detlef Horster. 1999. *Postchristliche Moral*. Hamburg: Junius.

Ocvirk, Karl Drago. 1998. *Med Narcisom in Kristusom* [*Between Narcissus and Christ*]. Celovec/Ljubljana/Wien: Mohorjeva založba.

Ocvirk, Karl Drago. 2000. *Lepo tveganje: hoditi z Jezusom danes* [*A Good Risk: to Go with Jesus Today*]. Ljubljana: Družina.

Ocvirk, Karl Drago. 2011. Evangelijski metanoeite za spravo v sekularni družbi [Evangelical Metanoeite for the Reconciliation in Secular Age]. In: Janez Juhant, Vojko Strahovnik, and Bojan Žalec, ed. *Izvor odpuščanja in sprave: Človek ali Bog?* [*The Source of Forgiveness and Reconciliation: The Man or God?*]. Ljubljana: Teološka fakulteta: Družina.

Pahor, Boris.2008. *Nekropola*. Ljubljana: MK

Palaver, Wolfgang. 2003. *René Girard mimetische Theorie*. Münster: LIT.

Pascal, Blaise. 1986. *Misli* [*Thoughts*]. Celje: Mohorjeva družba.

Pascal, Blaise. 2012. *Pensées*. London: limovia.net.

Pastoral Constitution of the Church in the Modern World = GS. 1966. Preface Nr. 1. In: W. M Abbott, J. Gallagher. *The Documents of Vatican II*, 199/200. New York: Guild Press.

Petkovšek, Robert. 1998. *Heidegger-Index (1919-1927)*. Ljubljana: Teološka fakulteta.

Petkovšek, Robert. 2004. *Le statut existential du platonisme: Platon dans l'analytique existential de Heidegger*. Bern – Berlin: Peter Lang.

Pettigrew, Thomas F. 1997. Personality and Social Structure. Social Psychological Contributions. In: Robert Hogan, John Johnson and Stephen Brings, eds. *Handbook of Personality Psychology*, 417-438. San Diego: Academic Press.

Piper, Annemarie. 2000. *Einführung in die Ethik*. Tübingen/Basel: Francke.

Pipes, Richard. 1995. *A Concise History of the Russian Revolution*. New York: Vintage Books.

Plato. Politea. 2013. http://www.gutenberg.org/ebooks/1497. accessed 29.6.2013.

Pope, Leo XIIIth. 1879. Circular Letter Aeterni Patris. In: Denzinger-Schönmetzer (DS). *Encheridion symbolorum definitionum et declarationum der rebus fidei et morum*, 610-612. Barcelona, 1965.

Pope, Leo XIIIth. 2013/1891. Encyclical *Rerum novarum*; http://www.vatican.va/holy_father/leo_xiii/encyclicals/documents/hf_l-xiii_enc_15051891_rerum-novarum_en.html; acces. 18.8. 2013.

Pope, Pius XI.th 2013/1931 Encyclical *Quadragesimo anno*; http://www.vatican.va/holy_father/pius_xi/encyclicals/documents/hf_p-xi_enc_19310515_quadragesimo-anno_en.html; acces. 18.8.2013.

Pope, Pius XI.th 2013/1937. Encyclical *Mit brennender Sorge*. http://www.vatican.va/holy_father/pius_xi/encyclicals/documents/hf_p-xi_enc_14031937_mit-brennender-sorge_en.html; acces. 18.8.2013.

Pope. Pius XI.th 2013/1937. Encyclical *Divini Redemptoris*. http://www.vatican.va/holy_father/pius_xi/encyclicals/documents/hf_p-xi_enc_14031937_mit-brennender-sorge_en.html; acces. 18.8.2013.

Potrč, Matjaž and Vojko Strahovnik. 2004. *Practical Contexts*, (Practical Philosophy, Vol. 8). Frankfurt/ Lancaster: Verlag.

Prijatelj, Erika. 2008. *Psihološka dinamika rasti v veri* [*Psychological Dynamics of Growth in Faith*]. Ljubljana: TEOF/Slomškova založba.

Prijatelj, Erika. 2011. Identities of Human Self: from the Standpoint of Guindon's Personal Identity Formation Approach. In: *Synthesis Philosophica*, Vol. 26, 267-281.

Pučnik, Jože. 2003. *Izbrano delo* [*Selected Works*]. Ljubljana: Mladinska knjiga.

Rahner, Karl. 1961. *Schriften zur Theologie* IV. Einsiedeln: Benzinger.

Rawls, John. 1999. *A Theory of Justice*. Oxford: University Press.

Rawls, John. 1993. *Political Liberalism*. Columbia: University Press.

Rescher, Nicholas. 1993. *A System of Pragmatic Idealism*. Volume *II: The Validity of Values*. Princeton: University Press.

Ricken, Friedo. 2006. “Mensch” und “Person”. In: Konrad Hilpert and Dietmar Mieth. *Kriterien biomedizinischer Ethik,* 66-86. Freiburg/Basel/Wien: Herder.

Ricoeur, Paul. 2004. *Memory, History, Forgetting*. Chicago/London: The University of Chicago Press.

Rifkin, Jeremy. 2009. *The Empathic Society. The Race to the Global Consciousness in a World in Crisis*. New York: Penguin Books.

Rolston, Holmes. 1987. *Science and Religion: A Critical Survey*. New York: Random House.

Ross, Jeffrey Ian. 2003. *The Dynamics of Political Crime*. Thousand Oaks/London/New Delhi: Sage Publications.

Rousseau, Jean- Jacques. 1954. *The Social Contract*. trans. Willmoore Kendall, South Bend, IN: Gateway Editions.

Russell, Bertrand. 1980. *The Problems of Philosophy*. Oxford: University Press.

Safranski, Rüdiger. 2010. *Nietzsche. Biografija njegovega mišljenja*. Ljubljana: Literarno umetniško društvo.

Schaupp, Walter. 2003. *Gerechtigkeit im Horizont des Guten*. Freiburg/Basel/Wien: Herder.

Schiller, Helmut. 1993. Einleitung: Die Wertethik in der philosophischen Diskussion der Gegenwart. In: Kurt Port, *Philosophische Schriften, Gesamtausgabe*. Esslingen: Port Verlag.

Schmitz, Josef. 1984. *Religionsphilosophie*. Düsseldorf: Pathmos.

Schmücker, Reinold, and Ulrich Steinvorth. 2002. *Gerechtigkeit und Politik: Philosophische Perspektiven*. Berlin: Akademie Verlag.

Schopenhauer, Arthur. 1991. *Preisschrift über die Freiheit des Willens. Ausgewählte Schriften*. Zürich: Diogenes Taschenbuch.

Schulze, Gerhard. 2003. *Die beste aller Welten*. München: Carl Hanser Verlag.

Schupp, Franz. 2003. *Geschichte der Philosophie im Überblick*. Hamburg: Meiner.

Sigmund, Paul E. 1996. Law and Politics. In: Norman Kretzmann and Eleonore Stump, eds. *The Cambridge Companion to Aquinas*. Cambridge: University Press.

Skrimshire, Stefan. 2008. *Politics of Fear, Practice of Hope*. London: Continuum

Slatinek, Stanislav. 2005. *Zakon, ki ga ni bilo* [*A Marrige that Wasn't there*]. Znanstvena zbirka Teologija, 1. Maribor: Slomškova založba.

Sloterdijk, Peter. 1999. *Sphären I. Globen*. Frankfurt: Suhrkamp.

Sloterdijk, Peter. 2010. *Scheintod im Denken, Von Philosophie und Wissenschaft als Übung*. Berlin: Suhrkamp (Edition Unseld).

Slovar slovenskega knjižnega jezika [*Dictionary of Standard Slovenian Language*, SSKJ], I. 2000. Ljubljana: SAZU Inštitut Frana Ramovša.

Smith, Adam. 1759/1970. *The Theory of Moral Sentiments*. London: A. Millar.

Smith, Adam. 1776/1902. *An Enquiry into the Nature and Causes of the Wealth of Nations*. London: Dent & Sons.

Smith, Dennis. 1999. *Zygmund Bauman: a Prophet of Postmodernity*. Cambridge: Polity Press (Key Contemporary Thinkers).

Snoj, Alojzij Slavko. 2000. *Pripovedovalna teologija – meje in možnosti* [*Narrative Theology – Borders and Possibilities*]. Ljubljana: Salve.

Snoj, Alojzij Slavko. 2003. *Katehetika: didakticna izhodišca religijskega, verskega in katehetskega pouka* [*Die Kathechetik: der didaktischen Grundlagen Religions, Glaubens- und Kathechetik-Unterrichts*]. Ljubljana: Salve.

Snyder, Thimothy. 2012. *Bloodlands. Europe between Hitler and Stalin*.New York.Basic Books.

Solomon, David. 2003. MacIntyre and Contemporary Moral Philosophy. In: Murphy Marc C., ed. *Alasdair MacIntyre*. Cambridge: University Press.

Sorč, Ciril. 2005. *Entwürfe einer perichoretischen Theologie Perichoretische Beziehungen im Leben der Trinität und in der Gemeinschaft der Menschen*. Münster: LIT Verlag.

Staehler, Tanja. 2010. *Plato and Levinas*. London: Rutledge.

Strahovnik, Vojko. 2009. Globalization, Globalized Ethics and Moral Theory. *Synthesis philosophica*, vol. 24, n. 2, 209-218.

Strahovnik, Vojko. 2009. *Moralne sodbe, intuicija in moralna načela* [*Moral Judgments, Intuition and Moral Principles*]. Velenje: IPAK, Inštitut za simbolno analizo in razvoj informacijskih tehnologij.

Suicide. http://en.wikipedia.org/wiki/Suicide. accessed 29.11. 2012

Svetelj, Tone. 2013. *Humanismo en le Contexto Secularizado de la Globalización: en Búsqueda de un Nuevo Humanismo*. In: El Humanismo y las Humanidades en la Tradición Educativa de la Compañía de Jesús. Guadalajara: ITESO, p. 113-133.

Šestov, Lev. 2002. *Dostojevski in Nietzsche* [*Dostoevsky and Nietzsche*]. Ljubljana: Literarno umetniško društvo: Literatura (zbirka Labirinti).

Štrukelj, Anton. 2002. *Leben aus der Fülle des Glaubens. Theologie der christlichen Stände bei Hans Urs von Balthasar*. Graz: Styria Verlag.

Štrukelj, Anton. 2004. *Kniende Theologie*. Zweite, erweiterte Auflage. St. Ottilien: EOS Verlag.

Štuhec, Ivan Janez. 1995. Die politische Situation und die Kirche in der Slowenischen Republik. In: Ingeborg Gabriel, ed. *Freiheit und Verantwortung der Kirche in der Gesellschaft*. Wien: Herold.

Štuhec, Ivan Janez. 2003. dersl.: *Europa- Beschützerin von Personen, Familien und Völkern*. In: Lorenzo Leuzzi and Cesare Mirabelli, eds. *Verso una Costituzione Europea*. Roma: Marco.

Tajništvo sinode Cerkve na Slovenskem (Secretary of the Synod in Slovenia). 2003. *Izberi življenje* [*Choose the Life!*]. Ljubljana: Družina.

Taylor, Charles. 1979. *Hegel and Modern Society*. Cambridge: University Press.

Taylor, Charles. 1985. Self-Interpreting Animals. In: *Human Agency and Language, Philosophical Papers,* 45-76. Cambridge: University Press,.

Taylor, Charles. 1989. Inwardness and the Culture of Modernity. In: Axel Honneth, eds. *Zwischenbetrachtungen im Prozess der Aufklärung. Jürgen Habermas zum 60. Geburtstag*. Frankfurt: Surhrkap.

Taylor, Charles. 1997. *Philosophical Arguments*. Cambridge, London: Harward University Press.

Taylor, Charles. 2004. *Modern Social Imaginaries*. Durham, London: Duke University Press.

Terrorism. http://ww.pbs.org/wgbh/pages/frontline/shows/binladen (accessed 20. April 2002).

The Church Today (*Gaudium et Spes* - GS). 1966. In: Walter M. Abbot. *The Documents of Vatican II*, 183-308. New York: Guild Press.

Torell, Jean-Pierre. 1995. *Magister Thomas. Leben und Werk des Thomas von Aquin*. Freiburg/Basel/ Wien: Herder.

Trstenjak, Anton.1988. *Človek končno in neskončno bitje. Oznanjevalna antropologija* [*The Man, Finite and Infinite Being. Announce's Anthropology*]. Celje: Mohorjeva družba.

Truhlar, Vladimir. 1967. *The Postcouncils Catholic Ethos*. Celje: Mohorjeva Družba.

Truhlar, Vladimir. 1971. *The Catholicism in the Proces of Deepeness*. Celje: Mohorjeva Družba.

Uhl, Florian. 2010. Religion, Gewalt und Relativismus. In: Nikolaus Wandinger and Petra Steinmair-Pösel. *Im Drama des Lebens Gott begegnen. Einblicke in die Theologie Józef Niewiadomskis*. Wien: LIT.

Valéry, Paul. 1957. *Œuvres. Tome I*. Jean Hytier, ed. Paris: Gallimard.

Valéry, Paul. 1962. *The Outlook for Intelligence*. New York: Harper & Row.

Valéry, Paul. 1993. *Cahiers/Hefte 6*. Frankfurt: Suhrkamp.

Van Huyssteen, J. Wentzel. 2006. *Alone in the World? Human Uniqueness in Science and Thology*. Göttingen: Vandenhoeck&Ruprecht.

Vattimo, Gianni. 1997. *Glauben-Philosophieren*. Stuttgart: Reclam.

Vattimo, Gianni. 2004. *Filozofska karta 20. stoletja: Tehnika in eksistenca* [*Philosophical Map of 20th Century. Technics and Existence*]. Ljubljana: Sophia.

Veber, France. 1923. *Etika* [*Ethics*]. Ljubljana: Učiteljska tiskarna.

Veber, France. 1923. *Znanost in vera* [*Science and Religion*]. Ljubljana: Tiskovna Zadruga.

Veber, France. 1934. *Knjiga o Bogu* [*There Is a God*]. George M. Trunk, trs. Chicago: private ed. 1942 (the translation needs essential corrections). Celje: Družba sv. Mohorja.

Večko, Terezija Snežna. 1995. *Divine and Human Faithfulness. General Observations and the Place of the Concept in the Psalms* (With the Cooperation of J. Krašovec), *Biblische Notizen*. Beihefte 10. München: M. Görg.

Večko, Terezija Snežna. 1998. Saul - the Persecutor or the Persecuted One? In: *The Interpretation of the Bible: The International Symposium in Slovenia,* 201-214. Jože Krašovec, ed. *Journal for the Study of the Old Testament*. Supl. Series 289. Sheffield: Sheffield Academic Press.

Vetlesen Arne, Johan. 1993. Relation with Others in Sartre and Levinas. Assesing the Implication for an Ethics of Proximity, unv. Ms. Januar 1993.

Vetlesen Arne, Johan. 2005. *Evil and Human Agency*. Cambridge. UP

Virilio, Paul. 1977. *Vitesse et politique. Essay sur Dromologie*. Paris: Galilée.

Virilio, Paul. 1988. *La machine de vision*. Paris: Gallilée.

Voegelin, Eric. 1971. *Public Essays. Vol. 12*. Ellis Sandoz, itd. and ed. Baton Rouge: Louisiana State University Press, and London.

Wallach, Harald. 2011. *Spiritualität. Warum wir die Aufklärung weiterführen müssen*. Klein Yasedow: Drachen Verlag

Weber, Max. 1904. *Die protestantische Ethik und der Geist des Kapitalismus*. J. Winckelmann, ed. Gütersloh: Verlagshaus.

Weiler, Joseph H.H. 2004. *Ein christliches Europa: Erkundungsgänge*. Salzburg: Pustet.

Weiler, Joseph H.H. 2005. *Krščanska Evropa. Raziskovalna razprava*. Ljubljana: Claritas.

Welte, Bernhard. 1982. Über die verschiedenen Bedeutungen des Nichts. In: Welte Bernhard (ed.), *Zwischen Zeit und Ewigkeit. Abhandlungen und Versuche*. Freiburg (Br.), 43-50.

Winch, Peter. 1987. *Trying to Make Sense*. Oxford: Blackwell.

Winnicott, Donald W. 1951. *Transitional Objects and Transitional Phenomena*. London: Hogarth Press.

Wittgenstein, Ludwig. 1963. *Tagebücher*. Frankfurt: Suhrkamp.

Wittgenstein, Ludwig. 1976. *Tractatus Logico-Philosophicus*. Ljubljana: Mladinska knjiga.

Yuval-Davi, Nira. 1997. *Gender and Nation*. London: SAGE Publ.

Yuval-Davi, Nira. 2009. *Spol in nacija*. Ljubljana: Sophia.

Zečevič, P. Seraphinus. 1954. *Francisci Veber, Theoria de persona. Internum drama philosophi sloveni*. Montreal: Editions Franciscaines.

Zelger, Josef, ed. 1989. *Von de Wissenschaft zur Kunst. Ausgewählte Schriften von Gerhard Frey*. Innsbruck: Amoe.

Zimmermann, Rolf. 2008. *Moral als Macht*. Reinbek bei Hamburg: Rowohlt Verlag.

Žalec, Bojan. 2002. "Bartelj Ludovik". In: *Enciklopedija Slovenije* [*Encyclopedia of Slovenia*] Vol. 16. Ljubljana: Mladinska knjiga.

Žalec, Bojan. 2002. Meanings of Identity. *Anthropological Notebooks*, Vol. 8 – Issue 1, 117-135.

Žalec, Bojan. 2004. Veber on Knowledge and Factuality. *Acta analytica*, Vol. 19 - Issue 33, 241-263.

Žalec, Bojan. 2005. *Doseganje dobrega* [*Reaching for Good*]. Ljubljana: Claritas.

Žalec, Bojan. 2011. On Not Knowing Who We Are: The Ethical Importance of Transcendental Anthropology. In: *Synthesis philosophica*, Vol. 26, no. 1, 105-115.

I wish to express my thanks for permissions to publish some of these scientific papers:

1. Juhant, Janez. Catholic neo-scholasticism, modernity and post-modernity. *Bulletin ET*, 2004, vol. 15, n. 1, pp. 67-79.
2. Juhant, Janez. Autonomous person as the basis of ethics: man between modern and postmodern morality. In: Juhant, Janez and Žalec, Bojan (eds). *Person and good: man and his ethics in the postmodern world*, (Theologie Ost-West, Bd. 6). Münster: Lit, cop. 2006, pp. 17-35 – revised and ammended.
3. Juhant, Janez. Anthropological foundation of dialogue. In: Hünermann, Peter, Juhant, Janez and Žalec, Bojan (eds). *Dialogue and virtue: ways to overcome clashes of our civilizations*, (Theologie Ost-West, Bd. 10). Münster: Lit, 2007, pp. 33-45.
4. Juhant, Janez. Ethical dialogue as a link between philosophy, science, and religion. In: Juhant, Janez and Žalec, Bojan (eds). *On cultivating faith and science: reflections on two key topics of modern ethics*, (Theologie Ost-West, Bd. 9). Münster: Lit, 2007, pp. 13-33.
5. Juhant, Janez. On living with: dialogue as the way to the art of personal and common life. In: Beck, Ulrich, Juhant, Janez and Žalec, Bojan (eds). *Art of life: origins, foundations and perspectives*, (Theologie Ost-West, Bd. 14). Wien; Zürich; Berlin: Lit, 2010, pp. 49-59.
6. Juhant, Janez. The corporal desire as a problem. In: Juhant, Janez and Žalec, Bojan (eds). *Humanity after selfish Prometheus: chances of*

dialogue and ethics in a technicized world, (Theologie Ost-West, Bd. 15). Münster: Lit, 2011, pp. 17-27.

7. Juhant, Janez. Are victims necessary for the survival of mankind. In: Juhant, Janez and Žalec, Bojan (eds). *Reconciliation: the way of healing and growth*, (Theologie Ost-West, Bd. 16). Zürich; Münster: Lit, 2012, pp. 59-70.
8. Juhant, Janez. Political Crime and the Truth of Man. *Anthropological Notebooks*, Vol. XIX, No. 2. 2013.
9. Juhant, Janez. Appendix: Theology in Slovenia, INSECT: *International Network of Societies for Catholic Theology*: https://theo.kuleuven.be/apps/insect/page/87/ - 1. July 2013.